How to Take Care

How to Take Care

AN A-Z GUIDE OF RADICAL REMEDIES

Erin Williams and Kate Novotny

A TarcherPerigee Book

tarcherperigee

an imprint of Penguin Random House LLC
penguinrandomhouse.com

Grateful acknowledgment is made to reprint from "VI. Wisdom: The Voice of God"
in *Tropic of Squalor: Poems by Mary Karr*, published by HarperCollins.
Text copyright © Mary Karr. Reprinted with permission.

Most TarcherPerigee books are available at special quantity discounts for bulk purchase for sales promotions, premiums, fund-raising, and educational needs. Special books or book excerpts also can be created to fit specific needs. For details, write: SpecialMarkets@penguinrandomhouse.com.

Hardcover ISBN: 9780593541074
Ebook ISBN: 9780593541081

Printed in China
1   3   5   7   9   10   8   6   4   2

Book design by Erin Williams and Laura K. Corless

This book is dedicated to everyone we've cared for,
and the people who've cared for us.

CONTENTS

You are holding a simple but radical guidebook for anyone who wants to learn how to care for themselves and others. In these pages, you will find tangible steps toward freeing yourself: slowly, tenderly, with self-compassion, and one moment at a time. Use this book however you need to—read straight through, skip around, or choose any page at random. Learn how to recognize trauma and its effects on the body, with tools and strategies to help you come back to yourself and live in the present. Discover the grounding of a clean sink and the joy of growing a flower from seed. Become curious about your inherent ability to heal.

We know these remedies work because they've worked for us and the people we love. We came to each other as friends many decades ago now. We've loved each other through substance abuse and recovery, three weddings, one divorce, countless jobs and careers, the birth of two children, and the birth of new versions of ourselves. In many ways, we've mothered each other, when no one else could or would.

"Mothering" can be done by a person of any gender, by people we are related to biologically or not, by people who gave birth to us, who were present at our births, or whom we've only just met. It is a role of nurturing, feeding, caring for, teaching, scolding, guiding, cuddling, and showing up when everything else is falling apart. When you are cared for by a parental figure, it teaches you how to take care of yourself. In societies and ecosystems where new families are nurtured, mothering and the exchange of parenting wisdom come naturally. In the industrialized, colonized, dysfunctional, misogynist, and racist society in which we live, mothering, self-care, and care of others are skills that we need to reclaim or, perhaps, learn from scratch.

There is no shame in being an unmothered child. It's not your fault or your failure, nor your parents', nor their parents' before them. At the same time, it's our responsibility to heal the unmothered parts of ourselves. The process is slow, wild, and strange. It requires humility and courage. Healing is possible, but it is up to us.

Before we start, it's important to understand what trauma is and how it can affect us.

When something harmful happens to us that we feel helpless to fight or change, trauma can result. We may experience trauma from a catastrophic event, such as war, sexual assault, or being the victim of or the witness to a violent crime. Or we might be affected by a series of less extreme but longer-term or chronic circumstances, such as having an alcoholic or mentally ill parent, living with financial stress or housing instability, or having our needs neglected as young children.

Like you, we are human beings who have survived trauma, and we love and care for other survivors of trauma. Trauma can be personal and subjective or passed down in family lines (intergenerational) and systemic; what matters is that when we experience or relive a traumatic event, we feel trapped in that moment. In *The Body Keeps the Score*, psychiatrist Bessel van der Kolk explains that when our fight-or-flight response is "thwarted," our stress hormone levels stay high and don't fall back to baseline. This causes us to feel extreme "agitation and panic" long after the event itself, sometimes for no apparent reason. Trauma lives outside of space or time—there is no end to the perceived threat—and the language centers of the brain struggle to describe it.

As a nurse and doula, Kate has learned a lot about trauma by listening to birth stories of friends and clients. One person may have had a near-death experience, but because of the care and support they received, their sense of autonomy remained intact and the experience was not traumatic. Someone else may have had what many healthcare professionals describe as a "good outcome" or a "healthy mom and baby," but because they felt trapped, in danger, or silenced, they experience post-traumatic stress disorder (PTSD). No matter how you respond, understand that it's not your fault—your body is doing its best to try to protect you.

Trauma, pain, and grief are not a sign of being broken but an experience of being human. It's an inevitable part of the human story. One of the first steps in addressing trauma is to recognize that it's real: an actual living experience in your body and mind. Maybe some of these symptoms of PTSD sound familiar: physical pain (migraines, body aches, chest pain, and stomach problems); nightmares, flashbacks, and repetitive thoughts; depression or anxiety; numbing or dissociating (going blank); and hypervigilance (always feeling on edge, never feeling safe).

Perhaps in the past, you found that no matter how many teas you drank, massage appointments you booked, or "self-care" products you bought, you felt like the pieces didn't fit. We felt like that, too. We learned that only in facing trauma and telling the truth—our whole stories, even the dark or shameful parts—can we become free.

Let's begin.

A

is for...

Ancestors

In our longing to heal, we must trace the thread from the dark forest where we are lost in the trees. Many of us don't know our family histories beyond our grandmothers: their birthday cakes whose colorful candles we blew out, the smell of their perfume, the photos and objects they passed down. We don't always know much about our ancestors—the towns they came from, the foods they cooked, the saints or spirits they prayed to—because so many of them fed their cultures into the furnace of American industry. More recent generations traded intuition for ambition, ceremony for consumption, wisdom for technology. Frameworks for responsively raising our young, community connection, self-sustenance, and true medicine were lost to the American Dream.

To acknowledge your ancestors is to become curious about your family's origin story. We inherit so many elemental traits, but when the truths of our roots remain shrouded in stigma and shame, it takes more work to excavate and understand them.

Therapist and storyteller Genevieve Slonim teaches us to ask our mothers: "How were you born?" This question can be a portal to reclaim the memories we long for.

In *My Grandmother's Hands*, Resmaa Menakem describes how trauma is not only personal but, if left unexamined, can fester to become familial and intergenerational: "Most of us think of trauma as something that occurs in an individual body [. . . but] trauma also routinely spreads between bodies, like a contagious disease." Many of us grow up exclusively learning the paternal side of our lineage, beginning with their last names. Learning the stories and lives of our feminine elders, and their birth stories in particular, illuminates what has been lost. Intergenerational trauma flourishes in the silence of our grandmothers' untold stories. To interrupt that spread of trauma, we have to dig down to the roots of our family tree.

We have learned, in addiction recovery (Erin) and in caring for other people's bodies (Kate), that healing is not simply a cognitive activity. Since ancestral trauma lives in the body, our healing must include and activate the body, too. Grief and trauma are a spiral, like the double helix of our DNA, that expresses our specific physical existence and experience, and offers a threshold back to where the injury first occurred. We can repair the broken chains of our stories by embodying ancestral memories: learning to bake our great-grandmother's pie, visiting the small town where our grandmother gave birth to her first baby, swimming in the rivers of our mother's childhood. These are the full-body experiences that can transform our past and our future.

TRY

Ask your relatives if they know the answers to these questions:
- What were the circumstances surrounding your mother's birth?
- How did your grandmother's labor unfold?
- What does she remember? What does she forget?
- How was she treated during the birth? Was she taught to honor and embrace the physiologic and holy process of bearing life, or did she learn that birth is shameful, dirty, or dangerous? Was she taught that the "suffering" of birth was caused by the sin of Eve?

Adaptogens

We have a tendency to overcomplicate things when we should be searching for the easiest solution instead. That means we don't need to buy expensive essential oils if we can make an infusion or cup of tea for ourselves. We don't have to order exotic and extractive plant medicines if we can grow helpful herbs in our own garden. Sometimes all we need is to eat nourishing food and move our body. Sometimes what our body truly needs is rest.

With this least-is-best approach, adaptogens can become trusted allies. Adaptogens are nontoxic plants that help the body resist stress of all kinds, whether physical (life-induced stress), chemical (toxic substances and pollution in our environment), or biological (toxic microorganisms, including bacteria and viruses). These herbs have been used for centuries throughout the world, including in Traditional Chinese Medicine and Ayurveda. They support the stress response system, alleviating the burnout that occurs during periods of prolonged physical or emotional upheaval, and regulating hormone production and flow. On our healing path, adaptogens walk with us as we ground and rebalance our central nervous system. Herbalist and nurse Stephanie Portell recommends taking them for several weeks, then gauging your body's response.

Anyone can become their own and their family's healer. Herbalism belongs to us all, just like CPR and basic first aid. Every time Kate learns to grow or use a medicinal plant, she does a little victory dance. It might not look like much, but every homemade remedy is a huge deal for a kid raised on microwave dinners, frozen bagged vegetables, and bubble gum–flavored amoxicillin. Learn about the plants that are accessible to you, that grow native in the environment where you live, or that you can grow yourself.

If you have any medical conditions, consult your care provider, an experienced herbalist, or a Traditional Chinese Medicine or Ayurvedic practitioner who can work closely with you to develop an individualized plan of care.

ASHWAGANDHA ROOT (*Withania somnifera*): Ashwagandha root, which grows in temperate climates, is a calming adaptogen that supports healthy sleep. It can be taken as a tincture, either placed under the tongue or added to a cup of tea. Ashwagandha powder can be combined with molasses and warm milk (either dairy or plant-based) and any other warming spice you like (cinnamon, ginger, nutmeg) as an iron-rich beverage before bed.

ASTRAGALUS ROOT (*Astragalus membranaceus*): Known in Traditional Chinese Medicine as the "yellow leader," astragalus root is considered a tonic herb. Take it to support your immune system and protect your organ systems from toxic stress. Make astragalus tea by simmering 1 tablespoon of dried, shredded root with 2 cups of water in a covered pot for 10 minutes. Strain through a fine-mesh strainer into your favorite mug. You can also add drops of tincture to food and drink.

A tincture is made by allowing the plant to sit in alcohol or glycerin; then the liquid is strained and preserved. Tinctures are consumed by the dropperful.

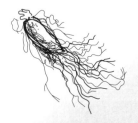

ELEUTHERO ROOT (*Eleutherococcus senticosus*): When taken consistently over time (try consuming it daily for a couple weeks) eleuthero is immunity-enhancing. Source it as a dried herb in bulk and prepare it using the same method as any other root (see Astragalus, page 5). You may also find it as a tincture.

GOJI BERRY (*Lycium chinense*): Goji berries have been used for centuries in Traditional Chinese Medicine as a nutritive tonic for the liver, kidneys, and blood. Rich in carotenoids and flavonoids, they support cardiovascular and circulatory health. Goji berries can be consumed dried or soaked, and can be added to hot cereals, smoothies, and snacks such as trail mix and granola.

Herbalist Brigit Anna McNeill cautions that bagged tea is not as effective as loose, but it can't be beat for ease, and our affirmation is that something is better than nothing.

REISHI (*Ganoderma lucidum*): Reishi mushroom is a vital fungus that's been used in Traditional Chinese Medicine for more than two thousand years. It is prized for its immune-supportive properties, for its use in treating reproductive conditions, and to balance the mind, consciousness, and emotions. Add the ground powder plus cacao to a morning latte for a warming, chocolaty pick-me-up.

Rhodiola root (*Rhodiola rosea*): Originating in the high-altitude mountainous areas across the northern hemisphere, rhodiola has a long history of use for treating symptoms of altitude sickness, for increasing physical endurance and stamina, and for resisting the effects of stress, including anxiety, depression, and fatigue. It can be brewed in the same method as astragalus and eleuthero, or taken as a tincture.

Schisandra (*Schisandra* spp.): Schisandra berry has been used for more than two thousand years to support the body's natural detoxification processes, and the liver, immune, nervous, and endocrine systems. The berries can be purchased dry, in bulk. To make a decoction: Add one ounce of dried berries, along with any other delicious flavors you like, such as rosemary and dried citrus peels, to 6 cups of water and gently simmer for 15 minutes, or until the color of the water changes. Strain and drink.

Decoction: a simmered infusion to help root-based medicines seep into water.

Tulsi (Holy basil; *Ocimum tenuiflorum*): Tulsi can be used for everything from reducing upper-airway dryness and congestion, to smoothing the edges of your temper, to improving digestion, to fighting off a cold. Try it as a tea by bringing 2 cups of water to a boil, shutting off the heat, and adding a palmful of fresh or more-potent dried herb. Let it sit for 10 to 40 minutes and enjoy. Tulsi can also be sourced affordably in prepared teabags.

Adaptogen Latte

INGREDIENTS

    1/2 cup milk (plant-based or dairy)

    1 tsp. honey

    Sprinkle of cinnamon

    1 heaping Tbsp. dried powder mix of mushrooms and adaptogens (about 100mg
        each): ashwagandha, eleuthero, and reishi

    Coffee brewed the way you like

DIRECTIONS

1. In a small saucepan on low heat, whisk the milk, honey, cinnamon, and adaptogen powder until all lumps disappear.
2. Pour coffee and blended adaptogen mix together, and enjoy.

Anger

Anger can be medicine, too.

Our patterns of emotional response to the outside world are ingrained from childhood. In dysfunctional households, in underresourced neighborhoods, or with absent parents or schoolyard bullies, we learn to hide, dissociate, go numb, or run away because it was how we survived. Anger is like that, too: a natural response to perceived danger or aggression. It evolved so we could defend ourselves. But when we hold on to it, it can make us sick.

We have to discharge our anger so we don't hurt ourselves and others. Sometimes we are filled with rage because someone cut us off at an intersection. Sometimes we are overwhelmed by righteous indignation at the world, at injustices of all kinds, and we have to release that safely, too.

It's difficult to hold space for our rage without letting it consume us. For so long, the rage may not have had a voice. Or maybe, sometimes, out of nowhere, all of that repressed emotion would explode out of us. As we heal, we learn that, just like fire, anger has its purpose. It can give us strength, it can nourish us, it can thaw us in our pain and stagnation, it can light the way. We can trust it, without letting it consume us. We must use it as a tool, instead of as a destructive force.

One of our tools is called a lamentation prayer. A lamentation prayer is when you scream, or cry, or get angry at God or the universe. You can say mean things. You can cuss. You can tell God whatever you think of Them, even if it's terrible. It's another way of praying. You can be grateful, or you can be angry. It doesn't matter, as long as you're communicating.

You don't have to believe in God for this to work. Before Erin knew how to pray or believed she was praying to anything real, one of her moms, Mary Karr, told her to give the middle finger to the ceiling fan or get pissed at the roof. Prayer is so valuable because it can provide relief and feelings of safety and security, even if you don't believe the prayers are going anywhere besides the ventilation ducts. This actually helps.

Refuse to swallow your anger, to let it burn you up from the inside out. Harness the fire, so it doesn't burn the forest down. It's *yours*, it comes from *you*, so it shouldn't be a tool the system uses to oppress you, hinder you, and inhibit your autonomy. Don't give the subject or object of your anger the pleasure of allowing it to disable you. Don't be afraid of it—trust it—but just like any other feeling, remember it's not in control. You don't exist to serve it. Use it to serve you.

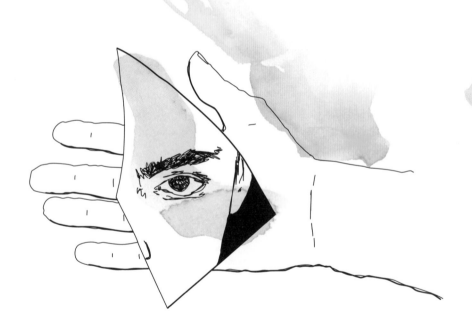

Antiracism

In *My Grandmother's Hands*, psychotherapist Resmaa Menakem describes how systemic racism wreaks havoc on every group within society, upon the bodies of Black, Indigenous, and other people of color enduring harm, and the bodies of white people who provoke it. No matter your background, eradicating the systemic racism and bias we've breathed, lived, and internalized is an essential task in our healing journey.

Eradicating our biases cannot be accomplished by reading a book (sorry!) or reposting memes. It's deep, nuanced, nauseating labor that requires a significant investment—for example, through professional antiracism coaching, where the coach is teaching from their lived experience, and adequately paid so they can care for the vicarious trauma they endure in this work. Getting personalized coaching is one effective strategy to move past the performance of antiracist behaviors and actions to expose the subconscious beliefs.

Our reconciliation process involves creating space (i.e., moving out of the way) for the healing of Black, Indigenous, and other people of color, supporting and honoring the creation of community circles, networks, and organizations where folks are allowed to exist and feel fully, reclaim their ancestral traditions, and safely process their pain, grief, and intergenerational trauma.

Regardless of race, ethnicity, or how we present to the world, we must become unendingly curious about our origin stories. We must learn the names of the demons that plagued our families. We must be willing to hunt, kill, and dissect them, even if it hurts. We must refuse to let these demons haunt our children, as they haunted our parents. There is no placating way to say this: white supremacy is evil, and it will poison every aspect of our lives unless we urgently and actively fight against it.

As Menakem writes, "Healing trauma involves recognizing, accepting and moving through pain—clean pain." This cycle of harm will end only when we face this pain head-on, take accountability, and begin the process of repair.

See Decolonize Healing (page 36), Reparations (page 118), and the Resources at the end of this book for reading materials, healers, and organizations to support and learn from.

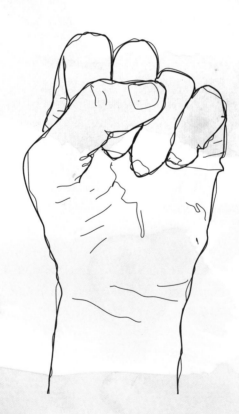

Ask for Help

Healing is not just for people who have their shit together. Healing is, most important, for people whose shit is falling apart. If your spinning plates are falling and breaking, then you're going to need extra help picking up the shattered pieces. Fuck martyrdom.

So many of us are raised to believe that we're supposed to be able to handle a million things at once: parenting, caring for sick or aging relatives, keeping our homes clean, earning a paycheck, providing emotional support for friends and loved ones. We're expected to do all that while processing the unyielding news of forest fires, hurricanes, tornadoes, wars, and injustice after injustice. The truth is that we're all sick and suffering, and none of us can survive alone.

If you are in crisis, say it out loud: *"I am in crisis."* A crisis may be spurred by some circumstance—a medical diagnosis, a house fire, or the birth of a child. It might be much simpler than that. It can be whatever and however you define it. As you heal, things will emerge from nowhere that will send you into a spiral, back to the triggering instant. Hold space for your recovery from that Worst Moment, as well as space for the times when memories of the Worst Moment are activated.

If you were the victim of a hurricane and lost your home, how would you continue to meet your basic needs? Apply those rules here. Ask for help from your friends and your community. Reach out to folks from your church, synagogue, mosque, or place of worship. Ask your neighbors. Be honest with your coworkers. Explain to your children's teachers what is going on. Tell the truth! Then accept the help that is offered.

This advice isn't meant *only* for when you're in crisis. Practice asking for help every day. Ask for help because you're tired or sad or overwhelmed. Ask for help because you don't know what's come over you. Even if you can technically do it yourself, ask a friend or a babysitter to watch the kids for an hour while you lock yourself in the bedroom and read a novel. Give yourself time for things that might feel unnecessary or unproductive, like watching TV or taking a walk. Respect your feelings, and ask for the help you want, even if you don't really *need* it. This is how we learn to honor ourselves and establish communities of care.

B

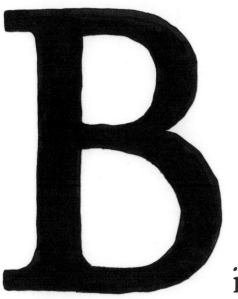

is for...

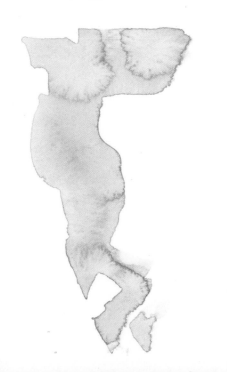

Body Affirmations

1.

I'm grateful to my body for keeping me alive, for being my aliveness. For my lungs, which inhale the smog of industry and still take deep breaths that perfuse my cells. For my heart, which beats despite its brokenness. When I run fast, it beats faster to pump blood to my muscles. It slows down when I feel safe, and when I need to rest. Thank you, liver, for metabolizing toxins, and kidneys and gut for excreting waste from my body. Thank you, immune system, lymphatic system, vascular system, and nervous system, for working together to keep me safe.

I'm grateful for my urges and food cravings, for how my body protects itself. (I'm especially grateful for carb-loading, in case I have to take off running or lift a car off a baby.)

Thank you, brain, for strategizing despite extreme exhaustion. For nurturing my memories of joy and beauty, despite my memories and experiences of trauma. I am more than my worst fears or memories. I am more than a body or a brain.

I am a safe place.

2.

I'm a living thing and my body's one job is to keep me alive.

My body is ever changing, sometimes bigger, sometimes smaller. Sometimes hairier, hungrier, softer. Sometimes tired, faster, slower, stronger, yet always capable, always resilient. My body has survived so much. What stories could it tell? Who it held, who it touched, who it chased, who it escaped, who it birthed, how it broke free. It stores all my memories, along the length of vessels and nerves, within cells, across fascia. It knows scars I can't see, the places where it healed back together to keep me alive. The last thing I should do is worry about how my body looks, especially to other people. I will tell how it aches, what it remembers, how it feels pleasure, pain, and joy.

My body doesn't have to tolerate people and things that squeeze it into too-small spaces. Despite everything that threatened it, hurt it, or tried to kill it, it has survived. It kept going.

It's okay if I don't know how to love my body yet. But I won't forget how much my body loves me.

Body Listening

Knowing the body is not an intellectual activity. There is no external resource you can memorize that is wiser than the simple experience of living in your body, no "expert" who can tell you how to listen to your instinct.

Some things are learned another way, through story, feeling, in a mother tongue. Some things are never spoken, only shown. The only expert, the only true whisperer to your body—of your body—is you. Your body is yours to learn. Even if you're a beginner to body listening, you still know your body better than anyone else, because you've been living in it all your life.

The body is a vessel and an altar. It's the place where we suffer most and where we hold every terrifying thing. It's also the place where we touch each other. Where we experience pleasure, love, and joy. Where we join blissfully in consensual sex and miraculously give birth to new life. Sexual violence, betrayal, PTSD, misogyny, and racism inhibit us from living safely in our bodies. Trauma causes us to dissociate from our bodies and their subtle messages to protect ourselves from intense physical or psychological pain. Thus, healing trauma, and reconnecting with our physical selves, must often be strategically relearned.

Our bodies are where we make a home for ourselves, or find our way back home. There's no rush to get there. It may take a lifetime, and that's okay. Body listening is a prayer, a remembering, a practice, a process, a reclamation. You don't need a Ph.D. to do it. You don't need wealth, health privilege, expensive vitamin supplements, or any other promises of capitalism.

Many of the activities listed in this book will help you ground yourself and find ways to relearn that your body is a safe and joyful place to be. Once you can learn to trust your body again, you can tune in to its quiet messages to you. These signals are your primal guide to healing, and only you can hear them.

Melinda

The Bolivia Principle

Sometimes we get so attached to the drama in our minds that we forget where we are. We could be snuggling with a loved one or witnessing some magnificent display of nature, but all we can think about is the coworker who said something mean or the guy who cut us off in traffic.

When Erin's friend Leslie was twenty-four, she decided to visit her boyfriend in Bolivia for a few months. But when Leslie got there, the same old problems in the relationship resurfaced. She called her mom and spent a long time explaining the intricacies of her complicated emotional landscape, what the boyfriend did or didn't do, the shame and suffocation she felt. Her mother acknowledged that it sounded like a difficult situation before adding, "I hope you're enjoying Bolivia. You might never get the chance to go back."

At the time, Leslie was annoyed by what appeared to be a dismissal of her Very Important Problems. In retrospect, she appreciates the lesson: Pay attention to where you are, because you might not get the chance to be here again. Get curious.

Our brains are constantly running, and we can get so caught up in the stories we tell ourselves, the drama, resentments, and anger, that we miss what's happening around us. We miss the common magic of living in the world. The Bolivia Principle reminds us to stop talking to ourselves in our heads for long enough to *notice* things: the shape of clouds, the texture of dirt, the dozens of types of squash for sale at an outdoor market. It reminds us that we can be present both for our Big Outrageous Feelings and for where we are.

Boundaries

Boundaries protect us. They can look like cutting someone toxic out of your life (temporarily or permanently), saying no to attending a family function, or asking someone to stop drunk-dialing you. It can mean telling your lonely, alcoholic father that you're not coming home for Christmas, even though it will devastate him. That you won't let your anti-vaxxer aunt come to your child's birthday party. That you're blocking your cheating ex's number even though you're still in love with them. You have absolute permission to disappoint and offend other people in order to save yourself and protect your heart.

When you love someone, it's hard to cut the rope that ties them to you if it means watching their boat drift away. We've loved so many, including those who've nourished us in the most profound ways. We've also loved people who harmed us. Sometimes, as with parents, we're both nourished and harmed by the same people. As we get stronger and wiser, the betrayals are less dramatic. We stand here, whole and healing, scarred and resilient.

No one else's comfort or priority should ever come before our duty to ourselves. We must care for ourselves first. Then we can extend help to the people we care for and love, who care for and love us.

We need to let go of anyone that exploits the tender or wounded parts of us, people we can't feel safe with, and people whose own trauma leads them to control and manipulate others. We need to let go of people pleasers, too, who couldn't find their way around a boundary if a good angel were leading them. We love all our fellow fuckups so much, but we can't continue to betray ourselves to make them feel better. When they're ready, they're welcome to walk with us.

A Meditation for Cutting a Motherfucker Loose

Close your eyes.

Your mind, body, and life are your temple. Picture the temple. What does it look like? What's the floor like? What shape is it? Does it have windows? What are the windows overlooking? What scents are floating through the air? How are you seated?

There are times when a motherfucker wants to set up camp in your temple. They drag a cheap, stained mattress in there, lie down on it as if they were born there, eat a hot dog, ketchup splotching on the sheet, watching TV at full volume. Who is trespassing into your temple? Picture them. What are they watching? Do you even want a TV in your temple?

Now, picture yourself. What are you wearing? White linen? Or, damn, maybe it's a purple crushed-velvet pantsuit. Whatever makes you feel radiant, powerful, comfortable, and alive. Stand your ground.

In this moment, you have returned to your true self: calm, planted upon the Earth, and knowing.

Open your mouth and speak.

> Listen, motherfucker,
> It's time for you to go.
> No matter what you do or say, I will not make myself small for you anymore. I will not bury my rage or desperation where it will burn me up from the inside out. I will let my anger out, and it will direct you, calmly and surely, out of my life for good.
> I may still love you, but I don't have to trust you. Love is a feeling. I listen to feelings, I serve them tea, but I don't let them control me. I can love you and let you go. I can love you and not give away my power.
> I belong to myself, not to anyone else.

When you're ready, let them go.

Breathe

As any birthworker knows, it's all about the breath. We love the medicine of breathwork because it is available to any of us at any moment: when we're in pain, when we feel a flash of anger, when we feel afraid, overwhelmed, or disconnected.

First, pay attention to your posture. Drop your shoulders. Point your chest upward toward the sky, like a bird preening. Give your heart to the sun! Your lungs extend from just under your clavicles to the lower edge of your ribs. Let them stretch to their full capacity.

Start with your belly. Push it out, let your body take up space. Feel your lungs expand. Admire them for their ability to grow. Fill your lungs from bottom to top, all the way up to your shoulders. Count to three as you are inhaling, pause, then count to three as you are exhaling. On the exhale, imagine yourself releasing everything you don't need. Toxic stress. Baggage you've been carrying. Old stories that no longer serve. The aches in your shoulders or low back. The worry, frustration, or fear. Slow your breath down. Even slower.

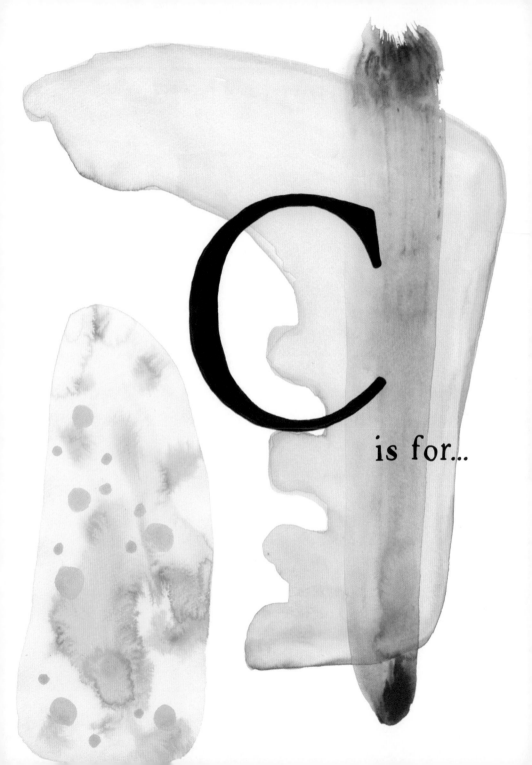

C

is for...

Calming Herbs

Kate learned the power of calming herbs as a postpartum doula. Anywhere from three days after a vaginal birth to six weeks after a cesarean, Kate would travel to her clients' homes, sit with them and listen to their birth stories, pray and lay hands over their bodies, rub their soft, squishy tummies, and brew them a bath. Calming herbs soothe and tend to the cold, dry, depleted parts of us. Their fragrances help release any tension we are holding, or allow us to sink into a deep, calming sleep.

To brew an herbal bath, bring a large pot of water to boil, shut it off, and toss in handfuls of dried herbs, such as calendula (pot marigold) petals, lavender tops, rosemary sprigs, and rose petals. Take a moment to notice the smell drifting enticingly through the entire home.

Discovering the plant medicine that resonates most with you is a personal and instinctive journey. Spend time with living plants if possible—visit a garden or a nursery, look for them in the wild, or grow your own. Smell them, touch them, witness them in their natural environment. Try different preparations (tea, bath, burning, oil) and see which plants call to your body and your heart.

CEDAR: Cedarwood oil calms the mind by reconnecting us with our higher, spiritual selves. Along with lavender, cedarwood essential oil can be applied to the big toes to help with sleep (with the caveat that for the first few nights it may produce vivid dreams). A couple years ago, we stopped burning wild sage, which is overharvested and overcommercialized. Try burning cedar, lavender, rosemary, thyme, or lemongrass instead to smoke-cleanse your home spaces. These herbs grow widely and can be grown in your garden or on your windowsill.

CHAMOMILE: These sunny flowers calm anxiety and tension and relieve headaches. The herb is safe for all ages, and may be consumed throughout pregnancy and the postpartum period. You've probably had it as an herbal infusion, and in the warmer months you can make it iced for a refreshing drink.

LAVENDER: This purple herb soothes anxiety, agitation, and restlessness. It also lifts our spirits and restores hope. Brew it with chamomile, or apply it in essential oil form to the temples, the back of the neck and wrists, or the big toes before bed.

To make an infusion: Add 1–2 cups dried herb, or 2–4 cups fresh, to a liter jar. Cover with boiling water and steep from 4–8 hours to overnight. Drink a cup up to three times daily, either iced, at room temperature, or reheated by adding more hot water or additional infusions.

LEMON BALM: Lemon balm reduces tension, melancholy, and restlessness by grounding an activated nervous system. It can be consumed as a tea or as a tincture. Make herbal-infused water with lemon balm, catnip, and peppermint by steeping a handful of leaves in a pitcher of filtered water in the refrigerator for a day. Strain and drink. (Use caution for those with hypothyroid. As with all herbs, please consult your care provider if you have any medical conditions.)

MOTHERWORT: Motherwort relieves agitation and/or rage, particularly due to hormonal causes, such as PMS. Herbalist Brigit Anna McNeill writes that it "eases tension and encourages a happy heart," and we find it is especially helpful when we are feeling abandoned or identifying with our wounded inner child. It can be taken as a tincture as well. Follow package instructions or consult an herbalist.

PASSIONFLOWER: This vibrant purple herb calms nervous anxiety and restlessness. Her cartoonish, curious flowers say, "Take yourself less seriously! Be free!" Brew in a tea with chamomile and lavender before bed to sleep tight.

See Adaptogens (page 4) and Herbal Baths (page 61).

Castor Oil Packs

After a decade of working as a night-shift nurse while also working as a doula, raising a toddler, and supporting her husband through law school, Kate started to feel sick. She remembered a naturopathic doctor who'd taught her about castor oil packs. Though in the past they'd seemed too messy and cumbersome to attempt, in her newfound desperation she decided it was worth a try. She applied the pack to her lower belly, piled her tummy with heated rice socks, and sank into her bed. The pack relaxed her whole body and made her muscles and connective tissue feel softer, squishier. The dull ache under her rib cage lifted. Her headaches lessened and hot temper subsided. The packs also relieved the "hungover" feeling that came from working the night shift. After that first experience, she was hooked.

How to Make the Pack

MATERIALS

Cotton or wool flannel, unbleached

Hexane-free castor oil

Cling wrap or something plastic or oil-impermeable, three inches wider than
the flannel when folded

Layers to absorb excess oil—old towel, a long scarf you don't mind staining

Heat source: Try two tube socks, filled with rice, knotted at the top, and
microwaved on high for 3 minutes, a hot water bottle, or a heating blanket.

A big blanket for your bed that you don't mind staining. If you really care
about your sheets, lay down a shower curtain with the blanket on top.

PROCESS

1. Saturate a piece of wool or cotton flannel with castor oil and apply it to an area of the body, then add heat. Before going to bed or after a sleepless night, use it below your right rib cage and over the liver area. Or, if you experience painful periods, try using one over your lower pelvic region throughout the month (three times per week), stopping once your period starts.

2. The first time, completely saturate the flannel. It will take a great deal of castor oil, perhaps an entire 6- to 8-ounce bottle. Pour the oil over the flannel, then gently massage the fabric until it is fully saturated but not dripping.

3. Cut a square of cling wrap slightly larger than the flannel when folded (6x8 inches square). Place the folded flannel on top of the cling wrap.

4. With your shirt pulled up, gently lift the cling wrap and flannel, and place it below your right rib cage.

5. Wrap the old towel around the pack and your waist. Wrap the scarf around your waist, then tie it on the side so you can lie down comfortably.

6. Lie down, placing the heated rice socks, hot water bottle, or heated blanket over your belly. Leave for 30 minutes to start, the longer the better, up to several hours. Use this time to nap, close your eyes, or focus on your breath. If you have to get up to answer the door or discipline a child, the scarf will hold the pack in place.

7. Remove the fleece and place it in a glass jar with a lid in your cupboard.

8. Remove the excess oil from your abdomen: scrub your belly and rinse. (We recommend Dr. Bronner's Pure-Castile Soap.)

You can use the pack three times a week, 30 minutes or more per day, while feeling symptoms. The fleece can be reused several times for up to two months. Tell your spouse, partner, or roommate not to be a jerk and "accidentally" throw it away.

See Eat, Pray, Liver (page 44).

Contraindications: Bleeding disorders (castor oil can thin the blood), same day surgery, and during pregnancy. Stop using once your period starts.

Create

Do it. Here.

Carbs

Some days, we just need a sandwich. Or french fries, crispy outside and fluffy inside, doused in ketchup. Or slices of pizza, with oozing hot cheese and pockets of sweet tomato sauce, flecked with basil. Sometimes it's potato chips dunked in sour-cream-and-onion soup mix that'll hit the spot. Or white bread toasted and spread thick with salted butter, sprinkled with cinnamon and sugar.

Two things can be true at once: A fresh juice of kale, grape, lime, cucumber, and romaine is divine. And sometimes we need a big bowl of $2 pasta smothered in butter and green-container "Parmesan." Make your inner child happy today. No shame, no guilt. Just delicious carbs.

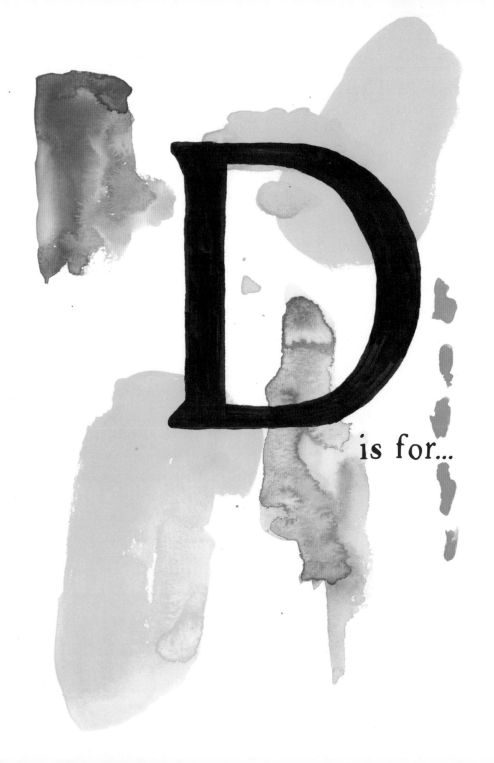

D is for...

Decolonize Healing

Western science teaches us that for a remedy to be "real," it has to be proven so in a double-blind, placebo-controlled, randomized clinical trial. This kind of thinking has been influenced by a colonized, racist, and patriarchal framework. The fiction of scientific objectivity was invented to serve white, cisgender, heterosexual men, while age-old Indigenous remedies were denounced as unscientific, old wives' tales, folk remedies, silly, foolish, dangerous, negligent, or criminal.

Some of these same "unproven" remedies and techniques have been repackaged and resold as "wellness" by affluent white cisgender people. This facet of white supremacy is known as *cultural appropriation*. Ancestral practices that have been co-opted under the "wellness" umbrella include sweat lodge ceremonies (Lakota tribe), ayahuasca and cacao ceremonies (Indigenous Central American cultures), use of cannabis (Afro-Caribbean cultures), smudging with white sage (several Native American cultures), yoga (Hindu culture), the body positivity movement (Black womanists), baby carrying/wearing (traditional African and Central American Indigenous cultures), and even the reemergence of homebirth midwifery and "attachment parenting" (Indigenous Mesoamerican, African, and southern Black cultures).

If we explore these modes of healing, we have a responsibility to uncover the past and strive toward repair. Nothing about this is simple or straightforward. We recommend investing in training by activist teachers speaking from their lived experience within the communities they represent. We must also become curious about our own healing traditions, and dive deeper into our family histories and ancestral origins, and reclaim our own lineages of healing practices.

In uncovering the old stories of what "medicine" is and who it belongs to, we make space for the miraculous, the magical, and the unexplainable. We learn that medicine is not the sole domain of Western doctors or exclusionary "gurus." Sometimes the most effective modes of care are freely accessible and can be found right near us—a plant growing in our yard, a harmony sung by two voices together, paint blooming across paper, or remembering an old way of doing things. Perhaps medicine is not only something written on a prescription pad or ordered from Amazon, but the acts of courage and accountability that bring us back to one another.

See Reparations (page 118) and the Resources section at the end of this book.

Mayte

Desperation

Opportunities for momentous change, for spiritual awakening, rarely present themselves when we're humming along in the status quo. It's when life shocks us, when everything around us falls apart, when we have nowhere left to hide and nothing to cling to, that we can become something new.

Sometimes the pain of having your heart broken feels worse than a death. Kate learned this lesson one Fourth of July when she heard a knock on her apartment door. The young woman standing there handed over a gold chain—Kate's husband's gold chain—and told her they'd been having an affair. That day, Kate left her first marriage and moved in with Erin. This was her rock bottom: sleeping on a futon, potato-chip crumbs stuck to her sweaty skin, in a loft with no air-conditioning. That's where she learned that rock bottom tends to feel quite bottomless.

Erin's rock bottom came four years later. She'd been a daily drinker for a decade, in and out of unfamiliar bedrooms, her guts caustic. That summer, a series of events brought her to her knees. Her grandmother, the most gentle, loving, and nurturing mom of her life, slowly died. Erin was robbed at gunpoint. Finally, she quit her job in corporate finance to become a prep cook at a taco shack, where she could drink during her shift. She became so physically sick from alcohol that her body felt blistered from the inside out. Rock bottom wasn't losing everything, it was losing alcohol. When she finally stopped, she lost every comfort she'd known, every solution she'd ever had.

Rock bottom feels like losing what you love the most. It's the moment when you say goodbye to your old self, the more innocent one that believes bad things don't happen to "good" people, that the world is stable and predictable, that you're in control. Like any good grief, it lasts too long and hurts like hell. But this is where you learn that at the end of all this pain, you can be free.

This is what we learned: Sit with your loneliness. Feel it rise, until it becomes a roar. You may long to be released, like a wave longs to break. Learn to hold still. As much as you want to run from it, you have to face it. Learn its shape. Do this without shame, resentment, or blame. If it feels like an earthquake, let it wreck what it wants to. Let it ruin what you no longer need.

Suffering is a door. Everything you ever wanted is on the other side.

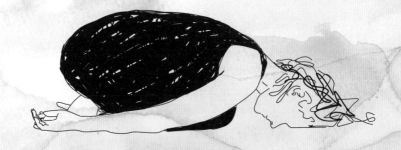

Do the Dishes

What if every once in a while, instead of thinking about what you *have* to do, you thought about what you *can* do, and how great just doing it would make you feel?

Take the dishes. A counter piled high with unsoaked dishes is triggering for Kate when she has spent the last couple nights at work. Some of her worst moments involve standing in the kitchen, screaming at the members of her family who've scattered and hid, even the dogs. *Do they want to live like members of a fraternity at a college where no one ever graduates?* Life is difficult sometimes, like how in dual-income, cisgender couples, women typically still handle the lion's share of household tasks like laundry, housekeeping, and meal preparation. A little mindfulness goes a long way.

How to Do the Dishes When You'd Rather Burn the Whole House to the Ground

Step One: (Or just skip ahead to step 2.) If you are planning ahead, or just trying to delay the inevitable, fill the sink with dish soap and hot water, and shove as many dishes in there as you can.

Step Two: Remove all the dishes from the sink, scraping food debris as you go. If you are lucky and have a garbage disposal, scrape the plates into the sink, otherwise into the trash or compost. Kate pours liquid with larger particles straight down the toilet, as if she lives on a farm or in Germany.

Step Three: Set the scraped dishes to the side of the sink, so you have an open space to scrub. Set a thick hand towel on the other side of the sink, where you'll dry the bigger pots and pans.

Step Four: Wash from cleanest to dirtiest. Scrub glasses or jars first, then silverware, then plates, then less sticky pots, then greasy pots.

Step Five: After you rinse, set the dishes on the clean towel, or into the dishwasher.

Step Six: Take a break to admire the size of your kitchen knives. Remember that simmering rage is also your superpower. You are unlikely to be a victim of homicide because anyone that tries to attack you will wish they were never born.

Step Seven: Connect with your breath. Decrescendo your slamming of the kitchen doors, your clattering of the dishes. Notice how beautiful it feels, as your filthy and cluttered kitchen slowly becomes cleaner, sudsier, and more organized. Start to think that you actually might like living here.

Step Eight (extra credit): Dry the dishes and put them away. That hero you've been waiting for? Turns out maybe it's you.

E

is for...

Eat, Pray, Liver

There will be periods in our lives when we have to dissociate from our bodies in order to survive. We have to hustle to put food on the table for our families. We have to work a full-time job (or three) while going back to school to fulfill our dreams. We dissociate from our bodies by ignoring their needs and taking them for granted. Our bodily organs and systems perform miraculously every day, and so we expect them to continue. But prolonged periods of stress, trauma, and depletion affect them in subtle, then more obvious, ways. When stress hormones stay high, our autonomic nervous system is hyperactivated, pumping blood and energy to our heart, lungs, and brain, so we are always ready to fight or take flight. Meanwhile, our parasympathetic nervous system—which governs rest, digestion, excretion, and sexual arousal—is neglected. Illness develops when stress continues long-term without any time to recover.

We can tell we're asking too much of our bodies when we feel symptoms of heartburn, irritability, anxiety, rage, stomach upset, bloating, difficulty sleeping, or PMS. For years, we've been running our bodies down through drinking alcohol, neglecting sleep, eating difficult-to-digest foods, and putting others' needs before our own.

The liver has hundreds of vital functions, from detoxifying the blood, to enhancing immunity, to regulating female hormone balance. Kate's Traditional Chinese Medicine practitioners helped her get her health back on track by teaching her to care for this important organ, and encouraging liver recovery through acupuncture, diet, herbs, and castor oil packs.

In Traditional Chinese Medicine, it is understood that each organ system is calibrated to a circadian rhythm. When it's that organ system's time, the body prioritizes energy and blood flow toward its repair and restoration: The gallbladder (11 p.m. to 1 a.m.), liver (1 a.m. to 3 a.m.), lungs (3 a.m. to 5 a.m.), and large intestine (5 a.m. to 7 a.m.) cleanse themselves and reset in the late-night and early-morning hours, when we should be asleep.

How to Love Your Liver

- Reduce consumption of substances that stress the liver out. Sugar, alcohol, dairy, trans fats, and processed foods are hard to process. If the liver is doing the constant work of digesting complex or inhospitable foods and substances, it can't focus on its restorative and regenerative duties.

- Consume foods and drinks that your liver loves, such as:
  - Coffee, which is hepatoprotective! (*Hepato* = liver) It may even reduce the risk of liver cancer and chronic liver disease. Cheers.
  - Leafy greens, cruciferous vegetables (broccoli, cabbage, cauliflower, Brussels sprouts), beets, carrots, and chives. Baby greens (kale, arugula, spinach, bok choy) can be added to soups for an additional boost.
  - Blueberries, goji berries, grapefruit, and strawberries.
  - Flaxseed, pine nuts, walnuts, and sesame seeds. Add flaxseed to smoothies, pine nuts to homemade pesto, chopped walnuts to oatmeal, and sprinkle sesame seeds on salads or stir-fries.
  - Cayenne, garlic, onion, vinegar, and turmeric. Consume turmeric freshly ground or dried to season, hot, and along with a good fat (like coconut or olive oil) and black pepper for maximum absorption.

- Consume herbs your liver loves: dandelion root, burdock root, and milk thistle seed. Brew a store-bought tea ("detox" tea blends often include liver-loving burdock, dandelion, and ginger). Add burdock and dandelion root to cooked polenta for breakfast; or sprinkle freshly ground, whole milk thistle seed over applesauce with cinnamon.

EMDR

EMDR (eye movement desensitization and reprocessing) is a type of psychotherapy that can relieve the symptoms of PTSD more quickly and effectively than other modalities (like talk therapy or CBT), sometimes in just a few sessions.

It works by facilitating better processing around traumatic memories and reorienting painful memories with new information. This allows for new learning and integration, which desensitizes emotional triggers. In an EMDR session, a licensed therapist will guide you to follow their hand with your eyes while recalling a traumatic memory. This may trigger the same kind of neural mechanisms that are activated during REM sleep. The brain becomes able to process overwhelming memories in a new way, and healing sets in quickly.

We've met so many people who have shared personal stories of how EMDR has helped them move through traumas, including sexual assault, medical or birth trauma, loss of a loved one, or recovery from an abusive relationship. Studies consistently demonstrate that most trauma victims are no longer diagnosed with PTSD after only a few sessions.

Once you learn to talk to your mind, nervous system, and body this way, it opens the door to other healing modalities. One of Kate's relatives used EMDR techniques while riding her bike. She engaged her mind around the triggering thoughts of a bad relationship, and worked through them by focusing on the movement of the left side of the body, then the right, while stating her new beliefs: "I am safe. I am whole."

Why not try it for yourself? See Resources at the end of this book.

Escape Your Own Mind, Five Minutes at a Time

- Submerge yourself in water: pool, lake, shower. Even the act of washing the dishes, running warm, soapy water over our hands, can make us feel a little bit better. A little bit is enough for now.

- Sit in a dark room or under a shady tree, and pay attention to your breath. Turn off all screens and all artificial lighting and remember, you are *here*. You are *alive*. Your life may be a shitshow, but it's also a miracle.

- Break something. Caveats: not someone else's property, or something that would be costly to replace. Make sure there are no small children or animals nearby. Take something you were meaning to throw away—like a gift given to you by someone who turned out to be a sociopath—and smash it on the pavement.

- Go for a walk. Listen to something that calms you down and distracts you from your pain. If you use a wheelchair, have someone push you. It's okay if it's raining—that might feel good, and remind you of that scene from *Breakfast at Tiffany's.*

- Take a nap. Sleep all day. Sleep is free, it's not hurting anyone, and it's necessary for people recovering from trauma or in grief. When you're at rock bottom, sometimes your days and nights get mixed up, which makes sense, because just like a newborn baby, you are being reborn. If you want to sleep, sleep. If you can't sleep, do something else. Your sleep or lack of sleep is unrelated to your worthiness. Try taking oral magnesium before bed to relax your muscles, bathe with Epsom salts, or drink a cup of chamomile tea. Rub lavender and cedarwood essential oils on your feet right before you lie down.

See Calming Herbs (page 26), Do the Dishes (page 40), and Rest (page 120).

F is for...

Feel It All

Grief can consume us. Sometimes we feel like we can't stand up because the pain of the world is too much. Everything feels irretrievably lost. Sometimes we convince ourselves the solution is intellectual or practical. We try to outthink or outrun grief, concoct solutions that will free us if we can apply them right. Sometimes we'll do anything we can think of to escape the pain.

There is no spiritual tradition you can learn that will allow you to bypass grief. If you think that meditation, prayer, herbs, tea, crystals, money, drugs, youth, romance, sex, beauty, or running away will allow that, the universe will teach you better. Grief will slam into your body like a wave, and somersault you head over feet.

Kate's work brings her face-to-face with people's worst fears come true. She's learned that as long as we stick together—with at least one of us to feel, and one of us to witness—grief becomes a ceremony. When we sit with it, we learn that it can't sink us.

Take the cold, hardened, brittle, skeptical, catastrophic-thinking, grandiose, manic, ruminating, exceptional, selfish, miserable, traumatized, skittish, unresilient, achy, older-than-her-years, agitated, scolding parts of you, and hold them as gently as you would the parts you're proud of.

Take those bare, dying, dead, scarred, burnt, broken, intolerant, and withered parts of you, and *see* them. Present them to the light.

Feel it now, if you can. Be grateful your pain falls from your eyes and yowls from your throat. Don't let it get stuck in your body. Know that life is worth living. Weep now so that you can wake up tomorrow and seek joy. Your pain is part of the story, but it's not the end. The only way out of suffering is through.

Fuck It

Is your home eligible for an episode of *Hoarders*? Fuck it.

Have your kids watched four hours of YouTube videos of an adult playing with fidget toys? Fuck it!

Did you order delivery for the third night this week? Seriously, fuck it.

Instead of giving yourself a hard time for doing the things you're definitely going to do because you're in crisis and need more help than you've got, you could just *do them*. Do them—and don't tell yourself that you are a bad partner/roommate/parent/employee/person because of it. You are not bad. You are exhausted. Most days it feels like the entire world is falling apart. You have complete permission to have a messy home, to plop your supple-minded toddlers in front of questionable media because you need a break, to add Grubhub to your home screen.

Seriously, fuck it.

G is for...

Gratitude

Expressions of gratitude can help us feel better when we're low. Research demonstrates that gratitude may be associated with increased happiness and better health overall. But before we get into all that: a warning.

We need to differentiate gratitude from its cousin, toxic positivity. Toxic positivity is the stance that you should be "good vibes only" effusively positive rah-rah about every experience in life. But when your basement floods, you don't need to be delighted that your attic didn't. You can just be angry and sad that your stuff is ruined. You're not required to give thanks for the shitty, shocking things that happen.

If you take one lesson away from this book, let it be this: You cannot bypass grief. You have to wade through it, even if the water is knee-high and brown and in your basement. Everything does not, in fact, happen for a reason. Sometimes the things that happen are just terrible. Don't use gratitude as a way of avoiding your own pain.

That being said, gratitude can be a useful tool. Erin reaches for her gratitude practice (an email, letter, or journal entry) on days when nothing is really wrong, but everything is getting under her skin. Kate takes ten-second videos of tree branches moving and posts them on her Instagram stories. When we're in a sour headspace, reminding ourselves of what we have and how far we've come can soften the hard edges.

There's a saying in recovery that the quantity of our problems doesn't change when we get sober, but the quality does. Life is still hard, but it's different. Fifteen years ago today, Erin might have been blackout drunk in a stranger's bed, or eating bodega bagels for every meal because she ran out of money for real, nourishing food. Today her problems are that her daughter is difficult and she has to replace the rusty oil tanks in her house and that shit's expensive. Fifteen years ago, she couldn't have conceived of either the nine months of sobriety required to grow a baby or saving up enough money to buy anything more expensive than a bus ticket. Quality, not quantity.

With gentleness, we can remind ourselves of how far we've come. We can be grateful for a sunny day that's not too humid, a perfect, buttery croissant, the friend who called and asked how we were, childcare, a pain-free day, a new set of pencils, an ornate iced latte. We can be grateful for the things that aren't broken.

Garbage Television

There is so much great television nowadays: *The Wire, Breaking Bad, Six Feet Under, The Handmaid's Tale* . . .

When you are in crisis, please do not watch these shows.

Have you ever seen the Real Housewives? Get cozy and buckle up, because Countess Luann, who is not a countess, is about to get shitfaced on tequila and fall face-first into the bushes, *twice.* The Real Housewives exist solely to make you feel better about yourself. Even at rock bottom, you're probably not fucking up *nationally. On television.*

Other suggestions:
- *Love Island*
- *Dance Moms*
- *Married at First Sight*
- *Naked and* (Motherfuckin') *Afraid*
- Any show* where Nicole Kidman is rich and miserable (rich people are miserable, too!)
- Cooking shows,* knowing you have *no intention whatsoever of cooking or baking* (*Chef's Table, Barefoot Contessa, The Great British Baking Show*)

Movies*
- *How to Make an American Quilt*
- *How Stella Got Her Groove Back*

- *It's Complicated*
- *Flirting with Disaster*

Note: It is perfectly appropriate to rewatch shows or movies you've already seen. The goal is not to improve yourself whatsoever, but to relax your nervous system. Do not watch anything that triggers you. For Kate, this is anything on HGTV, because of redlining. For Erin, this is *Keeping Up with the Kardashians*, because of the way they eat salads.

These are not garbage. These are masterpieces.

is for...

Hear

Surround yourself with the sounds that soothe you. When you hear something that puts your soul at ease, pay attention.

Sometimes we're afraid of silence because it makes us feel lonely. But silence is just what we need. Turn off your phone, your TV, your need to be constantly distracted by other people's opinions or the latest, worst news.

Your cat purrs. Laundry tumbles in the dryer. A vinyl record crackles. Flaming wood pops. Your neighbor's wind chimes twinkle. Cicadas thrum on an August night. Waves crash. Soap suds gurgle down a drain. A clear river crackles over rocks. Water bubbles as you boil it for tea. Your child breathes in-out, in-out, in deep sleep. Thunder cracks. Raindrops pelt the window. Sheets rustle as you shift your body in your warm bed. The furnace hums. Take comfort in the minutiae of everyday sounds. Let them remind you that everything will be okay.

Herbal Baths

Herbal baths are like a magic spell that you can cast for yourself. They are helpful whenever you are feeling dry, depleted, and chilled, such as during the change of the seasons, after travel, or in periods of giving your life force extensively to others.

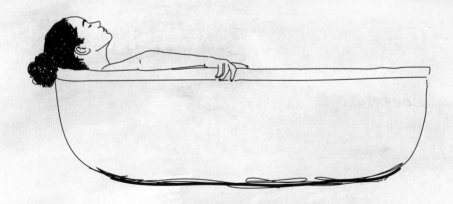

Herbal Bath Recipe

INGREDIENTS

Big pot of water

One heaping handful each of dried calendula, lavender, rosemary, yarrow,
    eucalyptus, rose petals, and/or peppermint*

Handful of salts: Epsom or pink Himalayan

1. Bring water to boil, then shut off and remove from the heat.
2. Add the dried herbs to the water. Stir and let sit, from 1–24 hours.
3. Bring the pot, the salts, and a large colander into the bathroom. Run the water in a freshly scrubbed tub, set the colander into the tub, and pour the herbal infusion into the colander. The infusion will immediately diffuse into the bathwater. (It's really magnificent to watch!) Remove the colander containing the used herbs. Sprinkle the salts over the surface of the water, and stir them in with your hands. This is a good moment to set your intention for the bath, whether you are drawing it for yourself or someone else. *Let this water relieve all tension and pain. Let the water wash away whatever ails.*

You can steep the used herbs once more for another bath if desired. Or toss into your garden or into a potted plant. If debris remains in the tub, remove after draining with a small dustpan and broom.

---

*To begin a personal apothecary, keep a jar of each or any of these herbs. When you are feeling depleted, ask yourself which one you are drawn to, by its scent, shape, or color. Lavender, rose, rosemary, yarrow, and calendula are soothing to irritating or wounded skin. This combination is safe even for newborns. Eucalyptus and peppermint open airways for those experiencing respiratory symptoms.

I is for...

Informed Consent

In our culture, we learn at a young age that doctors are experts who know what's best and we should follow their advice, even when it's counter to our intuition.

Intuition is *the lived experience inside your body*, not anyone else's advice. Not your chiropractor, your neighbor, or a conspiracy theorist your aunt reposted on Facebook. Since doctors are indeed highly trained and well educated, we often assume they understand our bodies better than we do. This is not always the case. A doctor might spend only a few minutes listening and diagnosing. No one should come between you and your intuition. Responsive care providers acknowledge this.

Some of us distrust physicians and healthcare workers to the point where we avoid seeking healthcare altogether, and for understandable reasons. There is a long history in the U.S. of doctors abusing their power in the name of research or the greater good, especially upon the bodies of women and people with uteruses, Indigenous and Black people, poor folks, and chronically ill or medically fragile people. Some of us have residual trauma over the ways we have been treated by physicians and healthcare workers in the past. Reclaiming our sense of bodily autonomy and our rights as patients can be a healing experience. Every human being is entitled to compassionate, ethical, and respectful care. Good doctors and nurses do exist, and you deserve to find them.

Kate says: As a registered nurse, if there was one thing I could remind you, it's that you have a voice. Your body belongs to you. You are not the passenger. You are the driver. The doctor, nurse, or midwife is not an authority figure. They are not your parents. They are not law enforcement. Though some of them forget it, their job is to serve you, and to help you become well.

The first relationship is the one you have with your body. It's sacred. The healthcare providers that care for your body must legally, ethically, and spiritually honor that. They took an oath to respect your autonomy, and to "first do no harm." Even if you are in need of care for any reason, you deserve that. Not only that, but illness is not your fault.

If you are anxious about seeking medical care, then bring a grounding visitor with you. Their job isn't to speak for you, but to be a witness. If you're feeling rushed, confused, or overwhelmed as healthcare providers are talking to you, or if you don't understand the procedure they're recommending, then ask them to slow down or explain it another way. When in doubt, ask, "Can you please give me five minutes?"

If your nurse isn't listening, then ask to speak to the charge nurse. If your physician isn't listening, then tell your nurse, "I do not consent." These are the magic words . . . *I AM AWARE OF THE RISKS, AND I DECLINE. Where do I sign?*

You deserve to understand what's going on with your body and your treatment options. You may consent to or decline them. You should always be the center of the healthcare "team." You are the first and most trusted expert of your body.

Inner Child

We are complex, mysterious beings. In our bodies, our cells, and our DNA, we carry memory, experience, and stories. Many of us experienced our first traumas during childhood. We may not be able to touch these memories consciously, but our bodies remember. The basic feeling of being safe, loved, nurtured, and nourished as very young children establishes the way we view ourselves and our world. Lack of this care makes its absence known.

We can't live fully as adults without gently holding our fragile inner children. The best part about healing your inner child is that it's *fun*. It is the pursuit of seeking joy. Perhaps you were thrust into adulthood far too young, forced to take on responsibilities or process mature information. Inner child work is about reclaiming lost innocence. It means hearing the voice of the little kid within us. Feeding them. Holding them. Comforting them. Listening to their fears. Letting them play.

We didn't realize how much our inner children wished to be heard until we raised our own kids. When we walked for hours with our squalling, colicky babies, when we learned to stay while our little ones expressed their urgent and unwieldy feelings, we learned to love and honor our inner children, too.

The inner child has needs. They need to be reminded to drink enough water, to be fed proper meals, not the crusts or crumbs left behind. They need to listen to music, to dance with their entire bodies, to paint with brushes and fingers, to make strange potions from plants. They need to receive little gifts and treats: a freshly baked blueberry muffin, a set of colored pencils, a new novel.

Our inner child needs affirmation and praise. They need to feel safe enough to be curious. They need someone to say they're proud of them. They want to celebrate life, whether that looks like learning the traditions of an obscure holiday, baking a dessert with seasonal fruits, or devoting a day to fun and play.

Maybe your inner child likes wave pools, campfires, fields of sunflowers, chocolate cake, or spaghetti and meatballs. Maybe they love being tucked into bed after a hot bath, playing with slime, painting with watercolors, or walking in the sun. Maybe they need to hold a baby animal in their hands, or laugh so hard they cry. Maybe they simply need to be told they're doing a good job.

What does your inner child want? Where do they feel the most playful? What feelings do they need to express? What makes them feel safe and whole?

Do that.

J is for...

Joy

For someone recovering from the stranglehold of control, we may believe we can be happy or content only if we can find balance. We may tell ourselves happiness is something we can *achieve*, if we can manage to become masters of the tightrope walk over our lives. We may have learned that we have to earn happiness—by having the right job, the perfect relationship, or an obedient, vegetable-loving child. Or maybe we can earn it through the material indicators of success: the house, car, good school district, and vacations twice a year. But moments of joy prove all that wrong. Joy isn't something you have to earn—it just lands in front of you, like a butterfly on a flower. Joy occurs in little moments, but you have to be awake to notice them.

Joy might be a dumb joke that makes you belly-laugh. It could be drinking iced coffee in your parked car when no one knows where you are. Joy can be a freshly made bed with clean sheets, a cardinal bobbing on the branches of the tree outside your window, a warm summer rainstorm you run into, barefoot. Joy belongs to you, and you always deserve it.

You don't need to be "healed" to deserve joy. You don't need to be "happy," "healthy," or in denial of the utter catastrophes befalling people you love, all around the world, all the time. Joy can be a ruckus of fireworks exploding, but it's also in the weeknight miracles: the soft cheek of a child resting her face next to yours, a purring cat in your lap, or a cup of tea that's exactly the right temperature. The key to joy is that it's not promised at any moment. It is a surprise, a gift, each time.

In our trauma, we want to grab something solid. Moments of joy happen even when we're at rock bottom, even when the ground beneath us feels unsteady. The trick is to be open. This can be a challenge when we're feeling low, resentful, and defensive. We close ourselves off then because we think we're protecting ourselves from further harm, but we're closing ourselves off from sweetness, too. The truth is that we don't know what's coming next. If we can open up, be vulnerable to joy as well as suffering, and surrender, we can see the bursts of light, even in the dark. When joy fades, as it does, we let it go. It will always come back.

Try to recognize the lush moments of joy that arise throughout the day. Keep track of them.

K is for...

Keep Going

"Keep going" is an affirmation we repeat to ourselves fifty times a day. When life feels unbearable, when merely continuing to exist, to be a human, to be a parent, to be in relationship with other humans who can be so awful and hurtful to one another, it makes perfect sense to want to give up.

Life falls apart. You might be wading through a quicksand of debt. You may be estranged from your family, with no fathomable way to reconcile. A substance you once used to numb your pain might be derailing your life. Your terrifying secrets might be aired out in public, for the judgment or entertainment of random strangers.

It is a very human experience to want to disappear. Your pain may lie to you and tell you that the people in your life would be better off without you. We know this experience well. It's a ditch we've both been stranded in before.

Two things can exist at the same time—you can want to escape, while learning how to stay. It is human to want to escape. Learning to stay—to wake up again the next morning, drink coffee, and approach the problem in a slightly new way—can be an act of heroism. When you want to disappear, any little thing you do instead of disappearing is urgent and brave. Getting out of bed, brushing your teeth, and putting on socks can be a miracle.

The one thing none of us need to carry is the shame of what's already happened. Lay down the burden of everything you no longer need: your shame, your regret, or what other people may think. There is nothing on this Earth that you could do or fail to do that would make you unworthy of forgiveness and love.

In these moments, keep going just a little bit longer. Do whatever you need to do to make it through the day, the next couple hours, or the next five minutes. If it becomes too difficult, break time into smaller pieces. There was once a mountain climber named Joe Simpson who fell into a crevasse and broke his leg, as he chronicles in *Touching the Void*. He hopped, crawled, and dragged himself down the mountain, the whole way counting to ten, over and over.

Life is sometimes like that. Though the mountain seems insurmountable, it's not so hard to count to ten. It is a sacrament, a holy act, to keep going.

Take a deep breath, and count to ten.

Kitchen Wisdom

There may be more healing in your kitchen cupboard than there is in your medicine cabinet. And what is there to lose? These remedies, with the exception of comfrey, are safe enough to eat.

APPLE CIDER VINEGAR (ACV): Buy a big old bottle of Bragg Apple Cider Vinegar—with the "mother," always—and before sitting down to a meal, drink a splash in a glass of water to assist digestion. Combine ACV with brown sugar to make an exfoliating face, body, or foot scrub.

COCONUT OIL: All crunchy moms know that dousing any physical injury in coconut oil is a surefire cure. Rub it on your newborn baby's bum to keep meconium from sticking to their skin. Use it as a moisturizer, as a lubricant for massage or play (but not with latex condoms), and for oil pulling, an Ayurvedic technique that may help with bad breath, inflamed gums, and teeth whitening. Swish a tablespoon of coconut oil in your mouth for fifteen minutes, then spit. Repeat daily.

COMFREY: Comfrey is an herb that soothes skin and brings down inflammation and swelling in injuries. Make a poultice by grinding a handful of fresh or dried herb and mixing it with castor oil to create a thick paste, and apply to inflamed or bruised skin. Kate once used this poultice to care for an inflamed tendon in her hand after an injury at work, and the swelling came down in twenty-four hours. Herbalists diverge on whether tea from the leaves should be taken internally, so proceed with caution (we say better safe than sorry here).

GINGER: To make a warming tea, grate fresh ginger and pour hot water over it. Ginger and cinnamon are two warming herbs that can draw energy to the internal organs, such as the womb, and are especially healing in the colder months. Add some roughly chopped knobs of ginger and whole turmeric to your broth, along with your bones or carcass, to make a fragrant, body-warming soup.

LEMON BALM: Make a poultice out of crushed lemon balm and aloe gel to apply to insect bites and bee stings. It is especially helpful at "taking the itch out" for those of us whose bee stings get very red and swollen.

MANUKA HONEY: Lovers of manuka honey, which is honey made from pollen from the antimicrobial tea tree bush, use it to bring down the heat of skin infections and irritations (in acne, impetigo, styes, etc.). It inhibits bacterial growth, even in drug-resistant bacterial infections. Apply it to wounds to prevent infection, even to perineal tears after childbirth. To boost your immune response when you feel a cold coming on, add a teaspoon to a cup of tea or drizzle on oatmeal.

MILK THISTLE SEED: Herbalists recommend milk thistle to support and strengthen the liver. Use it to ease stomach pain and indigestion when you haven't been treating your body nicely. Source whole seeds, grind them in a clean coffee grinder, and sprinkle over apples or applesauce.

ROSEWATER: Use rosewater as a spray to tone your skin; apply after washing your face. Seed keeper and farmer Rowen White also recommends using rosewater to soothe dry or irritated eyes. Using a medicine dropper purchased from a natural foods store, drip a couple drops into each eye, then lie down for a couple minutes and relax. Alternatively, soak gauze in rosewater and place it over your eyes as you rest.

L is for...

Light in Your Eyes

We cannot overstate the importance of getting natural light into your eyes on a regular basis. Sunlight lifts your mood, energizes your spirit, and provides you with nourishment in the form of vitamin D. We once met a woman who had five children. With the first four, she had crippling postpartum depression. The fifth baby had jaundice, and she was advised by her pediatrician to keep the baby next to a bright window, where sunlight could help break down the excess bilirubin in their skin. In those days spent in the bright light of the window, the mother noticed her mood lifting.

Aim to get outside for at least thirty minutes of full-spectrum sunlight a day, without sunglasses, year-round. This goal is especially important in fall and winter months, to help combat seasonal affective disorder (SAD). You can also sit in a sunny window and read, or purchase a light box, which may ease symptoms of SAD and increase energy levels.

Few remedies are as simple, free, and readily available as sunlight. We're just like plants: We need it in order to survive.

Love Is the Most Important Work You'll Do

Some days it feels like our most critical work—taking care of others—goes unseen. We cook food that gets eaten, or, worse, not eaten. We live in houses we are also trying to keep clean, a Sisyphean task in a household where all the adults work from home, the pets are poorly trained, and the children are creatively nourished (e.g., they commonly use a box of baking soda, a tub of glue, organic hand soap, and random household debris to make what appears to be a homemade bomb). Parenting is time and a half that never gets paid out.

This art of caregiving is not the exclusive work of parents. Each one of us gives care to our families, our friends, our colleagues, and our communities. We create moments, meals, memories. We make soup for a sick friend. We install plastic seats and handrails in our showers. We listen to our friend weep because she just got dumped, without telling her she never should've dated him to begin with. We cook for our loved ones, even if all we did was scoop mashed potatoes from a plastic container into a casserole dish. These constant acts of creation and love drop like blossoms all around us. Sacrifice and service to those we love always add more than they subtract.

We can nurture careers, passions, paintings, poems, dreams, essays, stories, and books, too. We can nourish new communities, new realities, and a new world.

Capitalism will tell you that something you do, create, sustain, or love does not matter if you don't get paid for it. But creation—genuine, defenseless, messy, vulnerable creation—is always an act of love. It has nothing to do with money or recognition, and whatever glory or disaster it finds out in the world is frankly none of our business. We create, and when we're done, we let it go. The world turns not because we *earn*, and certainly not because we consume. The world goes on because of our love, and the effort we give and the sacrifices we make because of that love.

Trust your love, first and always. Let it guide you. There may be days, weeks, months, or seasons when no one sees or appreciates this love. But the world couldn't exist without it. At the end of each day, you might ask yourself, "What did I accomplish?" The better question is, "How well did I love?"

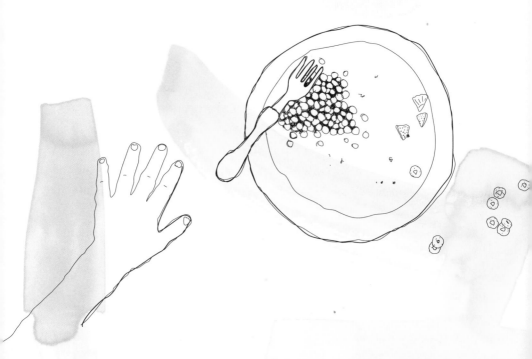

Love Yourself
Through the Worst Moments

It doesn't matter how you got here. Maybe someone you love has died, and no one cared to send you flowers, let alone make you dinner. Maybe you got cheated on. Maybe you overdrafted your bank account again. Maybe you're getting evicted. Maybe life is swirling all around, too much too fast, and you feel like you're slipping away. It might be physical, mental, or spiritual. But here you are, in the last place you ever wanted to be.

Some folks might call these "teachable moments." That's catchy and might resonate with you. Or you might be currently scream-crying in your parked car, and the idea that this moment is a "lesson" makes you want to take a baseball bat to a windshield. That anger is valid, and you don't have to listen to those people. Instead, know that wherever you are right now: You're okay. Maybe you're lying on the kitchen floor. As dirty as it is, as uncomfortable as it is, it's the only place you feel like being. The floor is your friend. The floor is trustworthy. There's no shame in feeling like you belong there. Let it ground you.

However ugly or hopeless you feel, with your messy hair, your unbrushed teeth, and your tear-soaked cheeks, *you are enough.* You may have fucked up, or had someone else fuck you up, but that doesn't change this fact. The worst moment is not your fault. When bad things happen, it's not because you're an awful person. It's because you're human, and being human is hard. It's not a reflection of your worthiness, but your humanity.

If you are feeling desperate, dark, or out of control (we've all been there), then first things first: Don't wait to get help.

See Keep Going (page 74), Meds (page 90), and Therapy (page 137).

Lower Your Expectations

We have certain things we do every day, week, or month. We shower, grocery-shop, make dinner, get the kids ready for school, go to work, change the sheets, clean the toilets, and put out the recycling.

When we are in a crisis or depression or just have too many things going on, we need to do less. Don't call it laziness, because it's not. Don't use it against yourself, but instead offer loving permission to *just do less.*

Here are some suggestions:

- Use paper plates and plastic silverware. The planet is burning and we should recycle, but just for now, let those standards drift. That empty salad bag from Trader Joe's is not make-or-break between us and mass extinction. It's Jeff Bezos's fault. Don't blame yourself for the consequences of end-stage capitalism.

- Make a grocery list and give it to a friend, get groceries delivered, or order curbside pickup instead of spending your precious time and emotional energy at the store.

- Drop off your laundry for wash-and-fold at the laundromat or use a pickup service. Ask your mother-in-law, your friend, or your neighbor Sally to come do your laundry, or fold and put away clean laundry, once a week.

See Ask for Help (page 13).

- If someone offers to help you clean, *say yes*. The trash needs taking out, and your pride doesn't pay the bills. If you have the resources, hire someone to deep-clean the kitchen and bathroom first.

Lower your expectations. A messy kitchen and a couple plastic forks do not make you a failure. They make you human, and hopefully a more rested one.

Meditation

Maybe when you picture meditation, you envision the formal practice, in a temple or at the end of a yoga class, of sitting still and emptying your mind of all thoughts. You resolve to try it, you download the app. You set the timer and sit. Your mind races. You go item by item through your to-do list before reminding yourself to *stop thinking*. Then the timer goes off and you feel like you didn't do meditation right.

You're not doing it wrong. There isn't one way to meditate. In the Eastern tradition, meditation might look like sitting quietly. In the Western (Aurelian) tradition, it's a practice of study and contemplation, of taking stock of your day (think journaling) or taking long walks in nature. Any practice you pick up is important only if it helps you. It can look like whatever you need it to.

When Erin was suffering from PTSD from sexual trauma, and feeling unsafe in her body, her therapist gently explained that our bodies have to *process* the trauma—we can't just shut down the feelings every time they arise. We have to show our bodies and brains what safety can look and feel like.

The therapist had Erin lie down on the couch and talked her through a simple guided meditation, like a body scan. Once she was relaxed and breathing steadily, the therapist encouraged her to feel whatever arose in her body. It was a practice of feeling feelings, the ones that are so undesirable or scary that we often reach for something to change them.

When our bodies are comfortable and safe, we can practice feeling the things we usually push away. We can surrender to them. At the end of the meditation, we're still safe. We show ourselves that feelings aren't facts; feeling scared doesn't always mean we're in danger. We teach ourselves to safely grieve. Over time, the feelings lose their power over us. Instead of shutting them down the moment they arise, we learn to sit with them, experience them, hold them up to the light.

Allow yourself to comfortably and securely observe how you feel without trying to change anything. Start slow, a few minutes at a time. Surround yourself with pillows and soft blankets. When difficult thoughts or feelings arise, the ones you'd normally try to shut down, remind yourself that your body is a safe place. Return your awareness to your breath.

See Pray (page 110).

Meds

When Erin had her daughter, the pregnancy was long and difficult, especially at the end. Her rib bones started going the wrong way and her body ached with needs she couldn't name. She was induced at forty-two weeks. For survivors of sexual assault with PTSD like her, birth can be triggering. She labored for fifty hours before having an emergency C-section. Her daughter was born during a blizzard. Her partner didn't have paternity leave. Erin lived in a town where she didn't know a single other person. The first two months felt like a war.

When the weather warmed, Erin began to take her daughter to storytime at local libraries and meet other parents. She thought everything was getting better, and it was. But then she started to feel anxious. She was familiar with the low thrum of worry, the spiraling thoughts that would eventually abate if she distracted herself good and hard. But the anxiety piled up.

She woke up one morning and saw her baby crying in the crib. Erin stood over her and sobbed as hard as she ever had, her arms limp beside her, unable to lift her wailing baby. She imagined throwing her baby and herself off the second-story balcony of their home. Then she went to a psychiatrist who specializes in postpartum depression. The doctor wrote a prescription. Erin had spent many bad years on many prescription drugs (it turns out psychiatric medications don't work when you mix them, daily, with near-lethal doses of alcohol). This time the drug worked. It saved her life, maybe her daughter's, too.

Meds are tricky. Years later, the same psychiatrist prescribed Erin benzodiazepines, drugs that would put her sobriety at risk. She declined, choosing instead to radically change her life, to fix the source of the problem rather than its symptoms. Sometimes this is possible, and sometimes it's not. Honesty and vulnerability are required to know the difference.

Remove any learned stigma in taking necessary medication to treat your anxiety and depression. There is no shame in doing this. Just because you take medication now does not mean you will have to take it forever. Or you may find you much prefer your brain on life-saving medication, and feel grateful, as we do, that SSRIs exist. You're rushing headfirst down the rapids. Now imagine someone throwing you a life preserver. Grab it.

Moms

Our biological mothers gave birth to us, marking us with a wild and unruly love for them, woven through with our unrealistic expectations. Some mothers don't know what to do with this primal love. It's a burdensome obligation, and they may try to shuck it off. Sometimes their humanness is hard for us to come to terms with, as we perceive their behavior to be a betrayal or a sin. No matter what kind of original mother we have (even if they are dead, or we don't remember meeting them), we can't help but love them. It may take us the rest of our lives to forgive them for failing to live up to that love. Some mothers are downright abusive, some manipulative, some neglectful. This complicates the terrain of our forgiveness.

In "A Kentucky of Mothers," poet Dana Ward writes beautifully about his many mothers, from Allen Ginsberg to "the Ella Fitzgerald cassette in the Honda." "Some mothers," he writes, "only last a season. Or a day. Or the life of the party." Ward reminds us that the story of a singular mother, the one that gave birth to us, is a lie. We were never meant to be mothered by a single person, but by an ecosystem. Throughout history, humans of all ages have been cared for by their community—by aunties, by neighbors, by high school teachers, by midwives, by coworkers, by sobriety sponsors, by nurses, by people we meet once and never see again. We can even be mothered by animals (like Brandi Carlile was, by her horse), by flowers, by trees, by music, by works of art, by spirits, by miracles, and by the natural storms of life.

Our mothers build us, nurture us, teach us, thrust us toward the light. They nag us, push us, slip us the secrets of survival in a difficult world. In *Women*

Who Run with the Wolves, Clarissa Pinkola Estés writes that instinctive mothers teach us how to protect ourselves from predators, how to reconnect to our innate inner compass of safety, and how to trust our fear.

Once we allow ourselves to be mothered by an ecosystem, we can forgive the shortcomings of our original mothers. We can acknowledge the gifts we received from them, and only them. There's an activist saying in Spanish that *"Mi mama me enseñó a luchar."* My mother taught me to fight. It may be the only inherited skill we need.

Who are your mothers? Did they spend a lifetime with you, a year, a day? Are they human, plant, or creation? How do you always keep them with you? How do you pass their legacy on?

Movement

There is nothing more natural than moving your body. Unfortunately, in our culture, physical activity has been yoked to so many negative things. Is there anything worse than the exhortation to "get your body back!," particularly in reference to postpartum bodies? Bodies grow, expand, shrink, get injured, recover, heal, adapt, and change. To tell you to get your body back is to tell you that your body abandoned you, which is the furthest thing from the truth. Your body is ever faithful, doing everything in its power to keep you alive and well, regardless of what crisis you are living through.

Trauma causes us to dissociate, and capitalism perpetuates this dissociation by placing the emphasis on how our bodies look, rather than how they feel. It is a trauma response to be obsessed with the shape of your body in the mirror, while feeling physically awful because you're depriving yourself of sustenance or punishing yourself with exercise routines that make you feel like you're having a heart attack. Go slower. What's the hurry? You have a lifetime to reacquaint yourself with your body and learn how you are really feeling, here, now, *in* it. Any rush to change is placed by external influences that don't care how healthy, grounded, safe, or alive you are, only that you might be interested in purchasing a new pair of jeans. FUCK. THEIR. JEANS.

The first step toward reclaiming your relationship with movement is to divorce it from the concept of "fitness," the goal of changing the number on the scale or your body into a specific shape. If you love pushing your body to the limits, more power to you, but we're not here to talk about that.

We are here to talk about how movement can heal you.

When you've been through a particularly difficult experience and are out of survival mode, you may develop symptoms of PTSD—especially if it was an abusive relationship, whether the abuse was physical, emotional, or psychological. Just like any other experience of PTSD, there are strategies that can reset your brain and nervous system into a state of calm and safety rather than hyperarousal.

Large, expressive movements, such as bike riding, dancing, yoga, running, and hiking, can profoundly nudge along your process of finding a home, a safe place, within your body. Yoga in particular has been shown to reduce symptoms of hyperarousal in PTSD and enhance the mind/body connection. Running and other vigorous exercise may help, too, by dulling our fight-or-flight response and honing our capacity to problem-solve. Movement allows endorphins, the hormones that dull pain and improve mood, to surge. No substances, experts, or special equipment needed. Just a pair of shoes and thirty minutes, and the relief of movement can become yours.

Movement is a love letter to your body. Walk out the door and find a long street, dappled with sunlight, filtered through the trees. Feel your feet hit the ground. Right, left. Right, left. Feel your lungs expand. Feel your sweat drip. That's your stress seeping out of your body. Thank your body for how it heals and protects you.

See EMDR (page 46).

N is for...

No

As caregivers, our first instinct is often to put other peoples' needs before our own. There are years when we are raising young children, and years of acute crisis (divorce, move, death of a family member, or serving critically ill patients during a pandemic) when life requires us to dissociate from our own needs. For a period, we can compensate. But after many nights, months, years of sleeplessness, terrible eating, and ignoring our basic needs, our brains, bodies, and emotional ecosystems will rebel. When we're totally tapped out, we still feel obligated to do the last load of laundry, play on the floor with our kids, or come through for a friend. Kate once made a lasagna for another family in crisis, only to discover that her own family had nothing to eat for dinner.

We often say yes when we should be saying no. Saying yes is not an act of love when we do it resentfully, or from a sense of duty outside of ourselves. We shouldn't say yes if it causes us to betray our own needs. There is a saying on airplanes and in addiction recovery: *Put on your own oxygen mask first.* Before you tackle the next task on your to-do list, check in with yourself. Are you hungry? Tired? Do you really have the energy for this?

Saying no is just as important as saying yes. The dishes can wait. Lunch plans can be postponed. Your employer won't burst into flames if you miss that meeting. Your toddler doesn't need to learn how to code today. This isn't an excuse to never do those things, but a method for learning to put yourself first.

Practice giving yourself permission to *do less.* Practice saying no even to things that feel important. Allot time each day to do simple activities of self-preservation: lie down, eat some fruit, take a walk, journal, meditate, take a nap. You don't need extra hours, just slips of time here and there. Take five in between work calls to close your eyes and clear your mind or sit outside in the sun. As you plan out your day, think about what you might feel like after lunch with friends. Will it fill your cup or deplete you? Do this *every single day.*

Because we live in a culture that venerates productivity, we often feel that we should exhaust ourselves until we collapse. We think that spending money on a babysitter or asking family to watch our kids so we can be productive and generate income is worth it, but asking for help so we can take a nap is not. We need to start valuing rest and restoration, not because they allow us to do more later, but because *we are worthy*. Rest is holy. You are just as worthy of receiving the care you offer to others.

See Rest (page 120).

O

is for...

Olfactory (Smell)

Trauma and grief are living experiences in the body. So is joy. Body listening means using all your senses to slowly and lovingly tip your physical experience away from fear and pain, toward pleasure and peace.

Smelling scents that remind us of good memories can increase positive feelings, decrease negative moods, disrupt cravings, and reduce physiologic experiences of stress, including systemic markers of inflammation. It will be different for everyone. Take a few minutes now to think about your favorite smells. They might include the smell of burnt wood just cut by a saw, bacon in a pan over a campfire, freshly ground coffee, a swimming pool in the early morning, your child's head, unfinished basements, the inside of Home Depot, or the pages of a brand-new book.

What smells give you a nostalgic sense of peace and joy? In the day-to-day, bring some scent into your home that evokes sunlit days, natural places, ease, and bliss. Find yourself somewhere that surrounds you with evocative fragrance. Stand outside and drink in the smell of spring rain. Stand in a grove of evergreen trees. Walk through a garden full of lavender or mint. Crush the leaves or blossoms between your fingers and breathe them in. This is a medicine, too.

P is for...

Peer-to-Peer Support

There is a special spiritual magic in helping someone through a problem that you have struggled with, when you take the wisdom you gained in the gauntlet and use it to protect someone in similar pain. There is also magic in helping someone release shame or self-doubt. When you help them shine a light into those dark spaces, the light within you expands, too.

Erin credits her decade of sobriety to that kind of peer-to-peer support. People who haven't suffered through addiction will never understand what it's like to devote your mind, body, and spirit to obtaining and consuming a substance that will kill you, that is killing you now. Her sober peers were the ones fielding her panic-stricken phone calls, dragging her ass to recovery meetings, buying her coffee, and listening to her horror stories. They were the ones telling her they'd been there and done that, too, normalizing her transgressions to deplete the shame.

The first few sober days and weeks feel like walking around without your skin on. Everything stings, feels foreign and strange: talking to people sober, taking the train sober, going to the movies sober, falling asleep sober. Other recovering addicts can guide you deftly through this time. They can love you until you learn to love yourself.

Once you get the hang of being awake all the time, confronting the unimaginable number of hours in each day, you can give others the care that you received. You can help travelers who are just starting out on the same journey. Call them, or answer when they call. Buy them coffee. Listen to them talk about their shame, and if it's safe to do so, tell them yours.

When we support others on the healing path we've already traveled, we're healing ourselves, too. We're showing someone desperate and raw that change and progress are possible, that we're living proof. We're showing ourselves how far we've come. You don't need to have it all figured out in order to hold and support someone else. All it takes is listening without interruption, unnecessary judgment, or unsolicited advice. Our time and attention are all that are necessary. Our presence is enough.

Plant Flowers

In a season of heartbreak, Kate set her attention on one dream: to plant a garden. She barely knew who she was anymore, let alone what she wanted. But she knew she wanted to move the garbage away from the lot behind her ground-floor apartment, she wanted to replace it with good dirt, and she wanted to plant flowers.

She ordered sixty bags of dirt and compost. She bought shrubs, ground cover, and bulbs to plant: grape hyacinth, bearded iris, tulips, and daffodils, which reminded her of her mother, Carole, and her grandmother, Cedetta. She chose flowers that promised to sprout early, when winter was waning. She needed something to look forward to. She read the little cards carefully, measured the distances, and buried the bulbs with her bare fingers. She prayed for them.

Part of her didn't trust it. She had been estranged from nature for so long. And when March came, the flowers took Kate by surprise. They bloomed.

How to Grow a Flower from Seed

Select a spot outside that gets at least six to eight hours of sunlight per day. If you're not sure, look where weeds tend to flower. If you are planting directly in the soil, wait for the last thaw, then choose your planting area and remove all weeds, otherwise the seedlings won't be able to compete. If you want your flowers to grow tall, enrich the soil with compost and peat moss, and fluff the mix until it's soft and airy. Sprinkle the seeds, per their instructions, over your fresh bed. Sprinkle dirt on top of them. Pack them down a little bit with your hands or enlist a child to gently pat down the dirt with their little feet. Water, and wait.

Portals

There are moments in life when our deepest transformation is possible. These are portals, or openings into the next version of ourselves. It's when we construct our cocoons and turn into mush. It may feel like we're lost, but really we're transforming into new versions of ourselves.

Birth is one such portal. No matter how much you prepare, how much you think you can control what happens, birth will teach you otherwise. Maybe you envision yourself as cool, calm, and collected. Maybe you picture yourself handling transition like an Olympian, or walking into the OR for your C-section like a radiant queen. Maybe you think you'll be the one that shows the hospital staff *how birth should be done*. Then when the first real contractions hit, you watch in slow-motion as your sense of self-worth dissolves like a cheap paper cup. Maybe you hardly recognize yourself, now a sweaty, puking mess, trying to bribe the staff to give you something better than Extra-Strength Tylenol. When it was Kate's turn to have a baby, she was dumbfounded, or maybe humiliated, to discover all of her experience guiding *other* people through labor did nothing to prepare *her*. After all those hours of supporting others, the books read, videos watched, and workshops attended, nothing eased that unthinkable pain.

This shock of discomfort happens in every portal, whether you're giving birth to a human baby, a work of art, an important goal, or a new life. A portal is any invitation that shakes us loose from the circumstances where we recognize ourselves: a job we're fired from, a relationship that ends, or a shameful failure that leaves us reeling.

It's natural to want to bargain with the universe to skip through the bad parts. But any labor nurse will tell you, birth of any kind is sweaty, unpredictable, bloody work. Maybe your true task is to learn how to say goodbye to the self you were before, so that you can be reborn.

When you are in the depths, and feel like the pain will eat you alive, sometimes all you can do is to hold on. Scream your head off, if you need to. If it hurts so badly you think you might die, you're not doing it wrong. Lose all fear of shame. Return, once again, to your breath. Though it feels like a hell you'll never pass through, remember there is no labor so powerful, no portal so harrowing, it can outlast you.

Pray

When Erin was getting sober a lot of people told her she'd have to start talking to God if she wanted to stay away from alcohol for good. This seemed impossible. God is for weak people, she thought. She even crossed out the word wherever it appeared in her program's materials. She mistook the refusal of comfort and security for strength. This is how she was raised. The only way out of the shame and discomfort of the last alcohol-induced transgression was more alcohol.

All addictions are like this: drugs, sex, work, shopping, food, hate. When we feel uncomfortable, we reach for something that will make us feel different, anything but this. The pain plays hide-and-go-seek. It finds a spot somewhere until we find it. If we leave it too long, if it runs out of places to hide, it finds us.

One of Erin's lowest lows was many years after her last drink. She was addicted to work, to how powerful it made her feel to be good at her job, the boss of something. At home, she was not the boss of anything, because she was a new mother. She stayed at work late, not because she needed the money, but the control. Her daughter had started to hit her anytime she got close enough to land a punch. She fought affection with violence because she didn't have the language to say *I need you and you're gone.* Erin pretended she needed to be gone, because being gone was easier than being uncomfortable.

Pain is the touchstone of spiritual progress. Some of us don't find God until we've exhausted all the other options. When Erin's suffering was so great she thought she might die, talking to God, real or not, didn't seem so embarrassing anymore. There was no illusion of rugged individualism left to uphold.

The Gods she knew about already didn't work for her. She thought about who God would have to be to help her with her daughter. She thought of her dead grandmothers, how they'd nurtured her, their offerings of mashed potatoes and warm loaves of bread. She felt their unconditional love in her body. She called God Susan, because she figured there were a lot of grandmothers with that name.

Susan, she said, *Susan, I can't do this. Susan, I want to run away.*

Stay here, said Susan. *You can stay right here.*

Erin learned to hold her daughter in such a way that she would not be hit. She repeated a mantra, *Susan help me Susan help me Susan help me,* during the tantrums. She learned to stay with her daughter even when she thought she had too much work to do. She learned to stay and let the pain pierce her heart. She learned that the job was not as important as she thought it was.

The tantrums get better and worse. Life is like that. The more Erin is attached to Susan, the more Erin is attached to her daughter. The moments between the tantrums get longer and easier.

In her book *When Things Fall Apart*, Pema Chödrön, a disciple of Susan, says that "Rather than indulge or reject our experience, we can somehow let the energy of the emotion, the quality of what we're feeling, pierce us to the heart." We can get to know that vulnerable place, to "lean in when we feel we'd rather collapse and back away." That's where we find God, too. Our weakness becomes our strength. When we let the pain pierce us, when we let God in, we can transform ourselves and our situation.

In mothering her daughter, Erin was mothering herself. As she provided a safe place for her daughter's pain, she built a place for her own. They taught each other how to soothe, how we can tend to the darkest corners of ourselves by just staying still.

The magnificence of prayer is that it helps us to withstand otherwise crippling discomfort. If we can sit with the pain, if we can feel it in our bodies, if we can let it crack us open and melt our hearts, we can heal the parts of us that are broken. We can learn how to show up for ourselves and other people in a new way. It brings us closer to our shared humanity, to profound humility, to real, earth-shattering empathy. It's magical stuff.

Erin ended up cutting her work hours by two-thirds, but not because Susan told her to. As Mary Karr wrote in her poem "VI. Wisdom: The Voice of God,"

> The voice never
> panders, offers no five-year plan,
> no long-term solution, no edicts from a cloudy
> white beard hooked over ears.
> It is small and fond and local. Don't look for
> your initials in the geese honking
> overhead or to see through the glass even
> darkly. It says the most obvious shit,
> i.e., Put down that gun, you need a sandwich.

Stay, God said. Learn how to stay.

is for...

Quitting

As children we're told that quitters never win and winners never quit. It took us too many years to figure out that this is bullshit. Quitting is a sacred practice.

Our work in particular often becomes part of our identity, and when we quit, we have to spin new rhetoric about who we are. Quitting can be painful and scary, the thrill of possibility commingled with the threat of the unknown. To quit mindfully, we must recognize and surrender to those feelings. Let them be heavy.

Erin has quit every job she's ever had (except the one where she was fired for not having sex with a manager). She's quit $9-an-hour jobs and six-figure-income jobs. She quit at least two dream jobs, because her dreams got bigger, and the jobs couldn't hold them anymore. When she quit drinking, drinking was who she was. That first, astringent sip always felt like coming home.

She got sober by attending free meetings where she heard both rape jokes and the voice of God. She met geniuses, houseless people, millionaires, millennials, and sick fucks. She met some of the best friends she'd ever have. Quitting drinking is the one thing that made everything good in her life possible. She learned how to ask for help and how to be of service to other people. She learned how not to drink long enough to carry a child. She learned that she was not the Absolute Worst Person Alive, which had been her perception of herself (this kind of pejorative grandiosity is sometimes called "terminal uniqueness"). In this big quit, and some of the big quits that followed, she learned that quitting what no longer serves us is how we *become*.

Make space for what's to come. Learn to love the parts of yourself that were told to be quiet, that were pushed too hard, that were exploited, overworked, or never thanked. Honor yourself by knowing when to stop. Quitting can be an act of hope.

R

is for...

Reparations

After all, if Black women were free, it would mean that everyone
else would have to be free, since our freedom would necessitate
the destruction of all systems of oppression.

—Combahee River Collective Black Feminist Statement, 1977

There can be no conversation about radical self-care without giving credit where
credit is due, to Black feminist thinkers, dreamers, and revolutionaries. As Audre
Lorde wrote in *A Burst of Light*: "Caring for myself is not self-indulgence. It is
self-preservation, and that is an act of political warfare."

If we want to abandon the manipulative, toxic lies fed to us by systems of
oppression in our racist, misogynistic, capitalist society, if we seek to reclaim our
lives and identities for ourselves, then we must uplift and fund Black, queer, war-
rior, poet models of care. These models imagine a future, not hard-fought through
suffering and martyrdom, but deliberately nurtured like any other care work—
through radical love, mutual aid, and truth-telling.

We must return power to the leaders that are making a new world possible,
a world where we can *all* become freer. We are all distinct and profoundly con-
nected. Thus, our individual healing can never be separated from our communal
healing.

If you have the resources, try funding the vision, leadership, and/or self-
sustenance of a Black or Indigenous birthworker, student midwife, or traditional

healer in your extended community. Ideas and affirmations are inspiring and helpful, but as the scholar and writer Rachel Cargle says, they must be followed by solidarity and action. Integrate these payments into your monthly budget. These payments are not a gift, but a gradual repayment of a debt owed.

For more ideas, see the Resources section at the end of this book.

Barbara and Glorious-Zoelle

Rest

The eight-hour workday and the five-day workweek are the inventions of Henry Ford and his little factory. It was Ford who decided we could have eight hours a day to rest, although what he meant was sleep. Rest is different. Rest is profound, radical, and anticapitalist. To rest is to unlearn the trappings of human value-as-productivity, of side hustles, the gig economy, moonlighting.

Rest is quiet, humble, personal. Especially for introverts, the mental loads of family and caregiving can be depleting. Sometimes we don't know the kind of rest we need until we find it. It's not always preceded by a bath and half a bottle of wine, though it can be. Rest can mean climbing a mountain, making spaghetti, snuggling your child and smelling their neck, doing the dishes, weeding the garden, reading. Rest can mean silence. When we find it, it feels like a drink of cool water after trudging up a mountain for hours.

Rest must be gentle, and done without a sense of duty. When we rest, we honor our better selves, the selves that are capable of healing from within, of becoming whole.

When we give, and give, and give of ourselves, eventually it catches up with us. We don't always realize how much life is asking of us. Processing any stress and trauma we're going through is hard on our organ systems, especially our adrenal glands. If we don't choose to rest, then our bodies will choose rest for us. Early on, this will present as exhaustion. But as time goes on and if we still don't listen, it will turn into chronic illness.

We have to ask ourselves whether we will choose to rest and enjoy it, or let our bodies choose for us, and become sick.

Questions to ask yourself:
- Why am I hesitant to give myself permission to rest?
- What am I losing by choosing to rest? Who am I *actually* hurting? What resource am I *actually* depleting?
- What internal dialogue is nagging me, telling me I don't deserve rest? How is refusing to let myself rest consistent with other harmful or self-destructive tendencies?
- How is my rest radical? How does rest revolutionize my life, and, by extension, the lives of my loved ones, family, friends, and community?

Repeat after us:
- There is nothing I have to achieve to make myself worthy of rest.
- There is nothing I have to do to prove my worthiness. I deserve to be here, just like the trees, flowers, rivers, and constellations.
- Rest is healing. Rest allows my body to do the work of repairing cells, replenishing organ systems, metabolizing nutrients, and excreting waste. Rest is productive and powerful.

When you're tired, rest. When you're scraped to the bottom, nothing else will work. Stop trying drastic measures. Just get naked and get into the tub—nothing fancy, just some hot water and staring at a wall. Getting everything done is not more important than being here. You're more important than anything you do or leave undone.

S is for...

Sauerkraut

The majority of cultures with ancient culinary traditions have some version of sauerkraut. This isn't your shelf-stable supermarket variety, cured with vinegar inside a jar. This sauerkraut is alive. In its most basic fermented glory, sauerkraut is cabbage, chopped thin, massaged with salt, topped with distilled water, and allowed to sit at room temperature until it begins to bubble and smell musky and delicious.

The problem with the standard American diet is that we consume many foods that inflame our digestive tract. We love them, they are delicious, it's okay. Our digestive tract is the gateway to absorbing nutrients and nourishment, but it also exposes us to harmful pathogens. Processed foods, refined flours, and concentrated sugars become particles and large molecules that pass into our bloodstream and distract our bodies' immune response. Sauerkraut is rich with *Lactobacillus* and other probiotic cultures, the same bacteria found in yogurt and over-the-counter probiotics. This blend of good bacteria blankets the length of your digestive tract, protecting your gut from foreign invaders and enhancing your ability to digest your food. But unlike yogurt, which contains milk proteins that some of us are sensitive to, sauerkraut can be eaten by nearly everyone, following any diet. Expensive probiotics capsules are mostly dissolved by digestive enzymes long before they can pass through the length of the GI tract. Meanwhile, the probiotics in sauerkraut, which is rich in vegetable fiber, remain intact, seeding good bacteria throughout the length of your digestive system.

Most health food stores sell live probiotic krauts and pickles. But why spend

$7 a jar when you can make it yourself for less than $2? All you need are clean quart-size jars, some clean breathable fabric or cheesecloth, weights, rubber bands, and time.

Sauerkraut

INGREDIENTS

A head of cabbage

An onion

Juice of one lime

Two heaping tablespoons of salt

1. Shred the cabbage and onion into slaw-size pieces.
2. Place slaw into a large bowl and squeeze or pour the lime juice all over.
3. Sprinkle salt throughout. Massage with your hands.
4. One cabbage will fill 2 quart-size mason jars. Pack the mixture into the jars as tightly as you can.
5. Pour distilled water (or tap water preboiled and cooled) until it covers the surface of the vegetables.
6. Weigh down with a clean rock or other weight and cover with fabric or cheesecloth held taut with a rubber band.
7. Wait seven days. When you remove the fabric, you will probably notice some mold growing around any bits of cabbage that floated to the surface and were exposed to air. Scoop these out and discard them.
8. Stir well, cover with the lid, and place into your fridge, indefinitely.
9. Add a spoonful to soup, use it to top your tacos, sprinkle over salads, or, once you've morphed into full hippie, eat it by the forkful as a snack.

See

In the Hindu tradition, there is a spiritual practice known as darshan, which means seeing an image of God. In more general terms, we can feel the presence of something greater than ourselves through our sight. Even though it requires nothing more than the act of seeing, darshan is a powerful form of worship.

Most of us passively consume so many images without contemplating how they affect our minds. What if we could learn to see more consciously? What if we tried to notice moments of grace in our daily lives?

See the color of the clouds in the early morning and at dusk. Each morning or evening, give yourself a single minute to watch the sky change. Tune in to the way the shifting colors make you feel. Sigh with relief that every day ends and a new one begins.

Ground yourself in the moment and time by witnessing. Some seasons are brief: The first bulbs poking up through thawing earth. The pale pink flowers of May trees in bloom, showering the ground like it's a wedding. The dark smear of the first blackberries. The haughty sunflowers of early fall. The flaming leaves of October. The first heavy snow, thick and smooth like buttercream frosting.

See the way sunlight saturates the leaves. Notice the difference between light and dark, light and shadow.

Everything changes so quickly. Give beauty your full attention. Make it last.

Service

Self-centered fear is the fear of what other people think about you, of not being enough. It's sharing your opinion in a meeting and then berating yourself for sounding stupid. It's interpreting a look from a passerby as judgment on your body type. It's obsessing about the meaning of a thumbs-up text from your crush rather than a written response. It's worrying that your selfie won't get enough likes. It's your concern that you'll never be good enough, smart enough, thin enough, strong enough, enough-enough. It's feeling like everything is all about you, and you're not looking too good.

Capitalism promises that salvation is only a click away. We all fall into this trap to some extent, but addicts especially. Many of us have learned that the way to escape our heartache is through consumption. Our self-centered fear is so urgent in these moments, so uncomfortable, we reach for whatever guarantees to make us feel different: a pill, a new pair of shoes, an Extra Value Meal, a $60 Pilates class where a friend of a friend once saw Reese Witherspoon.

Sometimes the solution has nothing to do with the problem. If you're angry, have a sandwich. If you're sad, take a walk. Sitting inside your mind and unraveling the threads of every possible meaning of that glance your coworker gave you won't help. Here's something that does: Stop thinking about yourself by being of service to someone else.

Research supports this: Volunteering can decrease levels of stress, chronic pain, and depression, and caring for people who suffer from problems similar to our own lights up the same brain circuitry as when we care for our children. In connecting with the suffering of others, in relieving their suffering in some small way, we validate and relieve our own pain. You don't have to march down to the nearest soup kitchen or pick fleas off a stray cat with a pair of tweezers, though by all means, feel free. Here are some gentler suggestions for when you have the energy to give:

- Pick up the phone and call a friend who's having a rough time. Listen without giving advice; just provide a safe space for them to vent or grieve. Don't talk about yourself.

- Drive to a friend's house and do their dishes or laundry. If they have kids, babysit so they can take a shower or go to a restaurant. Pay for their meal.

- Make someone soup.

- Write a letter. Tell a loved one why you're proud of them.

- Give up your seat on public transit. Let the woman in line behind you skip ahead. Hold the door open. Buy your coworker a cup of coffee.

- Give positive feedback. Tell a friend what a great job they're doing, even if all they've accomplished is to keep going.

Soup

Erin's Recipe

1 sweet potato
½ onion, diced
Olive oil
1 clove garlic
Ground turmeric
¼ cup brown rice
¼ cup lentils
Salt and pepper, to taste
Handful of kale or spinach
Handful of fresh herbs (such as parsley, dill, chives, or cilantro)
Fresh lemon juice, to taste

1. Steam a peeled, diced sweet potato in a little salted water until tender. Reserve the cooking liquid.
2. In a small pot, sweat the yellow onion in a big glug of olive oil. Add a minced clove of garlic and a hefty shake of turmeric.
3. Add brown rice and rinsed lentils of any kind. Stir the rice and lentils into the aromatics and then cover everything with one inch of water.
4. Bring to a boil, cover, and lower to a simmer. Cook for 20 minutes, or until the rice and lentils are tender.

5. Add in the softened sweet potato and the cooking liquid. Season with salt and pepper.

6. Add in ribbons of greens (like kale or spinach) and handfuls of herbs (like parsley, dill, chives, or cilantro). Taste again and adjust seasoning.

7. Finish with a little lemon juice to taste. Pour into a bowl and eat when it's warm, not hot.

8. This soup won't solve any of your problems, but it's delicious.

Kate's Recipe

1 whole free-range chicken (or bones you have on hand, such as ribs or ham hocks)

Herbes de Provence or other herb blend (see below)

1 onion

1 carrot

Other root vegetables

Milk thistle seed

A few garlic cloves

2 Tbsp. apple cider vinegar

1 bay leaf

PART I: MAKE BONE BROTH

1. Get yourself a whole chicken and a slow-cooker. If you eat meat, try to spend a little extra on animals that had a better-than-average life, in this case, free-range chicken. It's good karma. You can instead use bones, such as ribs, ham hocks, or any scrap you have left over.

2. Throw the meat into a slow-cooker so it's two-thirds full, and cover with water. Sprinkle with an herb blend such as herbes de Provence: something that includes sea salt, rosemary, thyme, sage, and/or dried garlic. Add

onion, carrot, root vegetables, something earthy like milk thistle seed, whole garlic cloves, a couple spoonfuls of apple cider vinegar, and a bay leaf. You do want the vinegar or another acid to help extract the nutrients, but don't stress if you don't have everything. Set it to cook on high for 4 hours.

3. Remove the bone and meat parts from the liquid broth and set aside in the fridge. Throw the bones, skin fully removed, back into the pot with the broth. Top it off with more water until the slow-cooker is three-fourths full.

4. Simmer for what feels like *forever*, at least 8 to 24 hours.

5. Strain broth into a large glass Tupperware container or jar, and when it cools down in the fridge or on the counter, skim the fat from the top and discard.

PART II: SOUP TIME

CHOICE A: FOR WHEN YOU HAVE SOME ENERGY

1. Sauté any combination of onion, shallot, shredded ginger, diced garlic, carrot, parsnip, or other roots in a swirl of olive oil at low-medium heat.

2. Add the sautéed veggies to a big pot with the broth and simmer chunks of potato, celery, and carrot, or slices of winter squash, for 40 minutes or until fork-tender.

3. Add faster-cooking veggies, like kale, dandelion greens, or bok choy.

4. Toss in the chunks of meat you had set aside in the fridge and simmer for 10 to 15 minutes. Shut off heat.

5. Finish the soup by adding any or all: throw in tender greens such as baby spinach or cilantro, a squeeze of lime, precooked rice or noodles,* a scoop of miso paste, or a spoonful of sauerkraut.

*If you are giving this soup to someone, keep the noodles separate so they don't get mushy.

CHOICE B: FOR WHEN YOU HAVE A TOUCH OF SLEEP DEPRIVATION OR
MILD DEPRESSION.

1. Ladle one serving's worth of broth into a smaller pot and bring to a simmer.
   Add leftover chunks of meat from the fridge. Cook the noodles from a
   package of cheap ramen. Toss in that flavor packet, too. Finish with baby
   spinach, live sauerkraut, and frozen peas.
2. Or do whatever you want. Good job either way.

Surrender

You can surrender to the wars waging in your own mind and body. It's about letting go of control.

When life gets tough, it can feel like everything that could go wrong does, all at once. Our natural response may be to tighten our grip around whatever it is we think we still control: our food, our family members, our schedules, our addictions. We may decide to try a restrictive diet, or shut down our social media accounts. It's not that those things can't be, under some circumstances, healthy, but when we're doing them as a reaction to the unmanageability of our lives, it can tighten the spiral of our panic.

The world can feel like a stage in our own minds, like the people we know are all actors, playing out life as we know it. We can become convinced that if everyone on stage just did *exactly* as we told them to, the show would be a success. Life would be okay. We can get so hung up on this kind of thinking that our expectations of others are really planned resentments.

Our bodies are so smart. When we feel threatened, we clench our jaws and tighten our fists, readying ourselves to fight some prehistoric animal. But unless we've climbed into the bear cage at the zoo, hardening our grip rarely serves us anymore (arguably, it wouldn't help much in the bear cage, either).

Surrendering can feel counterintuitive, but it works. When life gets especially messy, try giving yourself over to it. Loosen your grip, unclench your jaw, and let go. (Caveat: This is *not* applicable to people who are in immediate physical danger or victims of abuse.) Allow things to unravel and unfold, because that's what they'd do even if you had gone vegan or went on a house-mopping spree or bought a $700 pair of shoes. Give yourself permission to relax into whatever is happening and trust that you will survive it.

Things happen, and we don't always know whether they're good or bad. The poet Louise Glück writes that, "At the end of my suffering / there was a door." We don't know in advance where the doors are; we have to get through the suffering first. We can find our way there kicking and screaming, or we can accept the journey, surrender to it, and let it wash over and through us, without grasping for a handhold. It's the easier, softer way.

See Portals (page 108).

T

is for...

Taste

What are you craving? Hot, cold? Salty, crunchy? Warm, cooling? Spicy, sour?

If you were in the fully stocked kitchen of someone who knew you perfectly and wanted nothing more than to care for you, what meal would they prepare?

A bowl of olives? Apple slices soaked in fresh lime juice and sprinkled with cinnamon? Nutty cheese, crusty bread, and local honey?

A steaming bowl of simmered root vegetables in broth, with wilted leafy greens, thick rice noodles, and a scoop of tangy sauerkraut?

A plate of warm waffles with fresh berries and a smear of yellow butter, dripping with real maple syrup?

Picture the food that your body craves. What is your body asking for?

If you are hungry, then say it. What are you hungry for?

How is food an offering to the temple of your body? How can you express love and gratitude for your body with food?

Therapy

No matter how strong we are, sometimes we reach the end of our rope and need to ask for help. Depression and anxiety are liars. They make thousands of excuses about why you can't get help: You can't afford it, it won't work, and on and on and on. Don't spend another day feeling like you're drowning, and blaming yourself. Get help, now.

Some therapy relationships are terrible and traumatizing in themselves. Some can be helpful in moments, yet still not a good fit. Even if it feels demoralizing, try to nudge yourself to keep trying until you find someone who will listen to you, who makes you feel seen.

Kate's best therapist once asked her, "What's your dream?" He told her to keep it simple. He didn't ask Kate to plunge into the depths of her childhood trauma, or make plans for the next part of her life, or a year later, or to fix the many parts of her that felt broken. Kate's easiest dream was to plant a garden. And so she did.

Find a therapist, counselor, or social worker to talk to. We are here to tell you we've lived through rock bottom and survived, but words on a page will never replace the care of a real human who knows your history and can come up with a treatment plan. A plan! For you! To feel better! You deserve that.

Commit to at least four sessions. The alternative to taking care of yourself is much more expensive. Your mental health is an investment in your future and the future of your descendants. When you seek help, you become a role model for everyone in your life who looks up to you.

No matter how fucked-up you think you are, people can change. You can change. Therapy can expedite the process of putting back together the pieces that feel broken. It can give you the clarity to get back in communication with your inner heart. It can teach you skills you'll use when confronting triggering situations, stress, overwhelming feelings, or new traumatic events. It can teach you what to do in the middle of the night, when you feel utterly alone, or mid-panic attack, when it feels like you're crawling out of your skin.

Sometimes we need to practice to learn that we can change, heal, and grow. We need help to see that there is a future worth hoping for.

See Meditation (page 88) and Plant Flowers (page 106), and visit the Resources section at the end of this book for help finding local, cost-effective options.

Touch

Surround yourself with softness. Give yourself time each day when you let nothing touch your skin that constricts, restrains, or inhibits movement. If you wear a bra, take it off and fling it into the corner. Cover yourself with clothing that drapes effortlessly over your body. Take up space.

Feel the warmth and nourishment of a pool of sunlight on your arms and hands.

Lie naked in clean, silky sheets.

Create a nest of blankets.

Stick your fingers into dirt.

Feel the smooth, tender cool of new green leaves.

Rub the petals of a flower between your fingers.

Let the cool water of the faucet run over your hands. Let a hot shower cascade over your shoulders and back. Sink into a steaming bath.

Walk through a creek. Feel ribbons of water stream over your toes. Feel the mud squish under your feet. Feel the smooth surface of the rock as you rest your balance. Step gently.

Trauma-Informed Care

Trauma-informed care replaces the question "What is wrong with you?" with "What happened to you?" You don't have to be a professional caregiver to practice trauma-informed care. You can care for your children, parents, friends, coworkers, neighbors, or the strangers in the grocery store with a trauma-informed approach.

There are six core principles of trauma-informed care that apply to everyone involved, both caregivers and care-receivers:

1. Creating feelings of safety and security
2. Creating trust through transparency
3. Offering peer support
4. Leveling power differences for shared decision-making
5. Fostering empowerment and resilience
6. Recognizing ingrained biases and historical trauma

We used to think that there were some people (many, actually) that we would never learn to love, let alone like. The more we learn about trauma, the more we can understand the reason people act the way they do, even if it's belligerent, loud, defiant, dismissive, arrogant, rude, or hateful. As we become curious, rather than judgmental, we can see the intricacies of their humanity.

We've worked hard to soften the edges around the -isms that bias us against our fellow humans: our internalized racism, misogyny, homophobia, and trans-phobia, classism and ableism, and our fear of the differences between us. Intergenerational trauma and systemic racism are real. Our biases both cause and perpetuate trauma; they impact the ways we interact with one another, and fail to care for one another, every day. Becoming trauma-informed means we must learn our personal, cultural, national, and global histories to understand why we behave the way we do. We need to diagnose the illness so we can seek the remedy. Trauma is an infection that proliferates in dark, stifled places. Telling the truth, and exposing it to light, can allow these wounds to heal.

Trauma-informed care is radical because instead of saying "Hurt people hurt people, and that's just the way things are," we have a capacity and framework for change. What makes you feel safe, secure, and empowered? How can you offer safety, security, and empowerment to the people you care for directly, and your community at large?

Truth Medicine

Do you remember the first time someone asked you, "How are you?," and instead of answering "Fine, and you?," you answered with the truth?

Like most little girls, we were taught to be polite. When someone invited us over for dinner, we would eat all the food on our plate. We wouldn't raise our hands too often in class, even if we knew the right answer. We would try hard not to call our crush back "too soon." And when we were in emotional pain, even if it felt like we were dying inside, we would answer, "Fine, and you?"

When Kate had her baby, she realized that answering, "Fine, and you?" was no longer going to work. In her entire life up to that point, she had entertained thoughts of wanting to disappear. But once she had a wise-eyed, colicky baby to keep alive, disappearing was no longer an option. She didn't want to be a mother who never smiled back at her baby. She wanted the best for her daughter, or, at the bare minimum, better than what she'd had. "Better" meant that she would have to face her worst fears about being a mother.

Telling the truth is also critical to recovering from active addiction. There's a saying that "we are only as sick as our secrets." In the dark, our secrets morph into monsters. They grow and take up space. We feed our addictions to feed these monsters. When we start telling the truth, we hold our secrets up to the light. The monsters shrivel away. The urge to numb ourselves fades.

When we start to share our secrets we learn that they're not as bad as we thought or felt they were. When Erin was drinking, she often wound up in strange places with strange men doing things she wasn't sober enough to consent to. This brought on a lot of shame when she got sober and started remembering things. She had painful flashbacks that reminded her of moments she'd tried to suppress. But when she shared these awful memories with other women, every single one could relate. She learned to share her own story so it could help others, the way that their stories had helped her.

Like us, there might have been times when you needlessly suffered in silence with depression, anxiety, and paranoia. Perhaps what can finally heal your heart is sitting with other people, going through the same thing you are, and hearing their truth. Kate learned by visiting postpartum people's homes that the truth sometimes speaks for itself. Laundry piles on floors; toys, bills, and household objects collect in mounds; dogs bark, children cry, and mysterious smells waft. (Kate once found a pot of paella and a bong under a kitchen sink.) A messy home and an emotional human are not one and the same, though they can be.

We've learned to ask questions gently so the people we care for feel safe enough to tell the truth. In telling your story, even the sad, scary, dark, or awful parts, you soften. You open yourself up to change. It feels like sunlight streaming through a window, the clouds clearing.

Truth medicine is trusting yourself enough to be vulnerable with others, and, in doing so, becoming the kind of person others can trust, too. Being the cherished keepers of other people's truths shows that our own stories have power. Truly listening can change someone's life.

U is for...

Umbrella

Let's talk life skills. Perhaps, like us, you were the kid of a parent who put a key on a chain around your neck, handed you a Lunchables, pushed you out the door toward the school bus, and didn't reappear until dinnertime. (We love you, '80s and '90s moms who were just trying to Have It All.)

1. Pay attention to the weather. We know you're burned out. We know you never know what the fuck is going on. But people can learn new things. In the morning, after you make coffee and before you dive-bomb into the news of the latest signs of the Apocalypse, *check the weather*.

2. Dress for the season. Wear layers, so that when it gets hot, you can take off your sweater and let the sun shine on your arms without having to strip down to your underwear. When it starts pouring rain, you'll have a raincoat or an umbrella handy. Please, for the love of God, do not go out into the frigid cold wearing ballet flats.

3. Plan ahead. Get clothing and gear appropriate for the climate where you live. If you have hot summers, get a big hat, a well-fitting swimsuit, zinc-based sunscreen, and a pile of water bottles, knowing your family or roommates will lose most of them. If you have cold-ass winters (Hello, New York! Hello, Nebraska!), then get yourself a winter coat that looks like a sleeping bag and insulated, waterproof boots. Winter

coats go on sale in the springtime. You can learn to plan in advance for your own comfort and well-being.

4. Stop being surprised when it rains. Stop being afraid of inclement weather. If you remember your boots and coat, then a little rainstorm won't ruin your day. In fact, it might be just the relief you need.

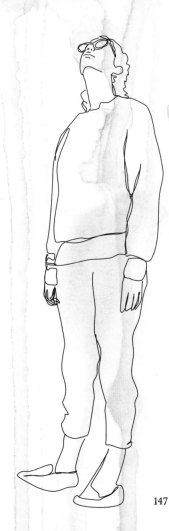

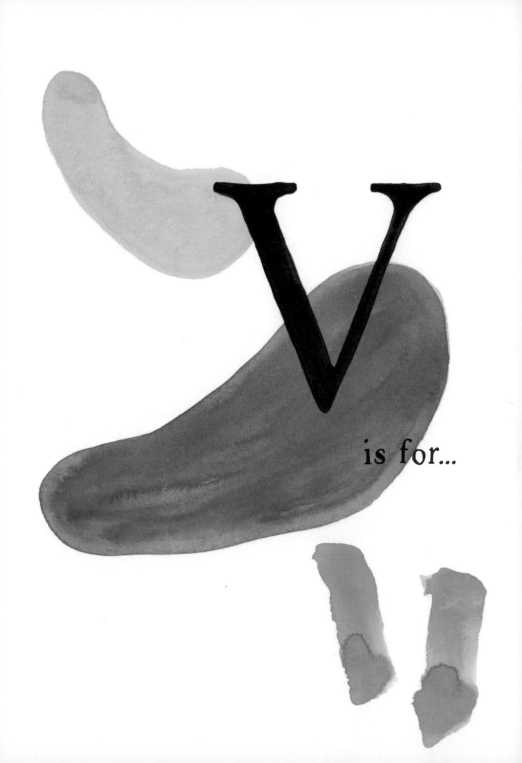

V is for...

Vicarious Trauma

Vicarious trauma is defined as "a process of change resulting from empathic engagement with trauma survivors." People who regularly empathize with survivors of trauma, such as healthcare professionals, can "begin to mirror the biopsychosocial effects shown by the victims of trauma."

For Kate, vicarious trauma was a portal. Early in her career in hospital environments, she helplessly watched as her clients and patients experienced birth trauma and obstetrical violence (unnecessarily harmful medical interventions). It was bad enough that she wanted to quit nursing and birthwork altogether. To carry on, she learned: to identify symptoms of vicarious trauma, to acknowledge when she needs help, and to give her brain, body, and nervous system the time and resources to recover.

Anyone can be exposed to vicarious trauma. It is all around us, whether it's police brutality, natural disasters caused by climate change, a global pandemic, gender-based violence, destruction of reproductive freedom and access to lifesaving healthcare (abortion), and social injustice. Here's how to become more conscious about how vicarious trauma impacts us:

1. Identify vicarious trauma. As nurses and healthcare professionals, we are taught to be stoic, unemotional, and professional. As birthworkers, we are taught to be empathetic but in control, and to put our own needs and feelings last. As human beings, if we witness traumatic things happen to other people, our brains and nervous systems think we are

experiencing trauma as well. Vicarious trauma can present as a rude or flippant attitude, rage or a hot temper, feeling numb with a flat affect, soul-deep fatigue, or thinking things are funny when they are actually fucked up and horrific.

2. Acknowledge when you need extra support. Go to acupuncture or cupping every week or two. Find trusted friends you can process your trauma with. Laughter is a coping mechanism, so create safe places to laugh with people who understand where you're coming from.

3. Give your brain, body, and nervous system time and space to recover, however tricky that is, or however long it takes.

See Ask for Help (page 13), EMDR (page 46), Meds (page 90), and Therapy (page 137).

Vulnerability

Being vulnerable, being open to emotional exposure, allows us to create meaningful connections with other people. Brené Brown defines vulnerability as "having the courage to show up when you can't control the outcome." It's time to shift your perception of vulnerability and acceptance of failure from a weakness to a strength.

Some of us were raised with parents who told us that vulnerability was a sign of weakness, who taught us to bury our feelings and put on a brave face. Some of us were convinced that failure at work or school was *personal* failure, *moral* failure, indicative of poor character and never being good enough.

Out of fear, we've learned to skirt vulnerability in remarkable ways. We want the quick fix, but not all of the luscious learning that happens from messing up along the way. Have you ever taught a child to ride a bike? They've got to fall, fall, and fall again, skin knees, bust elbows open. They cry and want to give up, so you kiss their forehead and hug them until they're ready to go again. Social media deprives us of the magic within the mess. When we curate our lived experience into neat little squares, we lose the nuance, the beauty, and the ache. In this version of ourselves, we are smiling and polished. Our homes are clean. Light filters in through a window on a houseplant. Someone clutches an artful latte in manicured hands next to a highbrow book they definitely haven't read.

All of this makes us feel lonely. It makes us feel unworthy because we haven't gotten a manicure in months, our skin is sagging, our houseplants have turned brown, and our couches are stained with cherry yogurt.

Try simplifying your concept of vulnerability, boiling it down to just one thing: We need one another. We need to *see* one another. We need to spend time together in real life. We need to spend time in one another's homes; stained fabric, cracked drywall, Magic Marker art, and all.

Throw a half-assed dinner party where instead of overspending to perform some sort of alternative life, you simply welcome the people you care about straight into the middle of your mess. Chipped dishes, paper napkins, sauce scorched to the bottom of the pan—bring them on.

We need to sit together and be brave enough to let ourselves be known.

W is for...

Wash Your Hair

Just do it. Not for anyone else. Just for yourself.

Wilderness

Being lost, like being happy, is not something we *are*, but something we *feel*. No matter what we learn about healing and recovery, there are times, moments, and situations that make us feel as broken and helpless as ever. Always remember that "heal" is a verb, because being a human means that we are vulnerable—to pain, to grief, to ways we've adapted to cope with living in a traumatic world. No matter how far we come, there are moments on the path of healing when we have to begin from scratch.

When you're feeling lost, it can be helpful to *actually* get lost. Getting lost in nature is one of the quickest ways to recalibrate your nervous system, heart, and soul when they're feeling especially fragile.

You can find a wild place even in the middle of a city, in a corner of the park where some trees have grown especially unruly. You can find it in a state park; most Americans live within an hour's drive of a larger chunk of public land. You can find it in a national forest. There are so many places where camping is low-cost or free. Look for the green patches on a map, and drive into them. Walk at least an hour, in one direction, to shift your consciousness and change your mood.

Safety first: When going in nature or seeking out wild places, trust yourself, pay attention to your surroundings, and keep your phone charged. If you're afraid to go into nature alone, invite someone to go with you. But know that there is a special magic in being quiet, turning off the language centers of your brain, and listening to the trees wave, the insects thrum, and the birds sing.

Wonder

So much of our pain comes from getting caught up in Who We Are. Children are constantly asked, "What do you want to *be* when you grow up?," as if *being* were a place—a static, unchanging thing. We mistakenly believe that adulthood means accumulating a pile of identities: sibling, child, spouse, professional, friend, citizen, parent.

There is safety in identifying with the seemingly unchanging parts of us. We need something solid to stand on, so we choose a platform: Survivor of Childhood Disasters, Woman Who Resents Her Husband, Hot Mess Mom, or Self-Sacrificing Friend.

The problem with fixed identities is that they're, well, fixed. They're like a dock on a shimmering lake with aquamarine water, reflecting the sky. We might stand on the dock and say, "This is where I live, this is *my dock*." But docks are stuck in place. We can marvel at the water and say that we understand the lake. But standing on a dock is nothing like paddling out into the middle of the water. It is nothing like standing in your tiny, rickety boat, feeling it slosh from side to side, then diving headfirst into the deep. In staying put on the dock, you miss the good stuff . . . the shock of the water. The sensation of floating. Your body's freedom, under the waves.

Some folks go to extraordinary lengths to change the story about who they are. They go on journeys across the world, travel for ten hours over flooded dirt roads, surround themselves with people whose languages they don't speak. They push their bodies to the limits, running ultramarathons, a hundred miles through deserts, down canyons and back up, in intense heat. They take vows of silence and fast for days. They take MDMA, psilocybin, and ayahuasca. These are all conscious attempts to untangle their rope from the dock, which sometimes work, and sometimes don't.

Film theory teaches that the secret to a compelling narrative relies on one non-negotiable: the protagonist has to change. This archetypal story is called the hero/ine's journey. The heroine's journey can be epic. It can involve rowing a four-woman kayak across the Pacific Ocean. It can be hiking the Pacific Crest Trail, alone, to process the death of your mother. It can be rushing into the room of a patient whose contagious disease has no known treatment and could possibly kill you.

Or it could be so much simpler and smaller.

It could be having an honest conversation with a parent who didn't meet your needs as a child. It might be buying your first new bike in fifteen years. It could be making an appointment with a psychiatrist six weeks postpartum, to get a prescription for life-saving medication when intrusive thoughts begin to take over. It might be trying EMDR, to brave a memory with so much power over you that it makes your sweat pour and your heart race. It might be learning to hear your inner child, and driving out of your way to get a chocolate-swirl ice-cream cone with rainbow sprinkles.

A Meditation

Find a comfortable place to sit, turn off your phone, and close your eyes.

The water is sparkling in the low afternoon sun, waiting to surprise you with its cool kiss. You're standing on the dock. If you can summon the courage to jump, you'll be blessed with the wild understanding that there is no separation between you and the water, the beauty of the lake and the beauty within you, the power of the healing depths, and the power to heal yourself. It doesn't matter how long you've been standing on that dock. Imagine the entire world out there, patiently waiting for you. Take a deep breath, and dive in.

X is for...

XXX

As a labor nurse and doula, Kate has learned to talk to strangers explicitly about sex. No whispering, no euphemisms. Only the facts, spoken plainly, without taboo or shame. There are a wide range of responses. She might be alone with a young couple, who clearly had sex to conceive this baby in front of them, yet when she asks them when was the last time they had sex (a mandatory triage question!), they blush and stammer a vague response.

Sex is something our bodies do, just like eating, sleeping, or sneezing. It takes some time, courage, and patience, but it's possible to reclaim sexuality for yourself, on your terms. The first step is seeing your body as *yours*, belonging to you, and not existing to serve anyone else's desires or needs for pleasure, scrutiny, or power. That may mean never having sex with another person again. It might mean learning to have an orgasm by yourself for the first time. It might mean buying a crystal sex toy and using it, gently, on your body (even if it never touches your sexual organs). It might mean studying the work of Betty Dodson and Annie Sprinkle, and becoming sexually radical as fuck.

So many of us, regardless of our identities or anatomies, have healing to do around our sexuality. Who can blame us? Our culture is ashamed and disoriented about human sexuality. When and if you are ready, your nurse is here to remind you: Orgasms are good for you. As you have probably read in any women's magazine in your dentist's office, orgasms relieve stress, quiet the parts of the brain responsible for fear and anxiety, reduce pain, and improve your mood. But sexuality doesn't begin and end with orgasms, or even our sexual organs. Sexuality is finding peace within your own body, your skin, and honoring what ignites your desire. Is it kissing? Holding hands? Having your crush touch your neck? Having your partner clean the kitchen? A well-fitting pair of jeans? Midday naps? Bass guitar? Cedarwood? Candlelight? Log cabins? Strength? Espresso? Honesty? Instead of viewing sexiness as something we *perform*, perhaps it can be something we seek, and admire, in ourselves and in others.

There is absolutely nothing to be ashamed about having a body that experiences desire, however that looks for you. Your body, your sexual self, is always worthy of your attention, respect, and care.

Y

is for...

You Are Never Alone

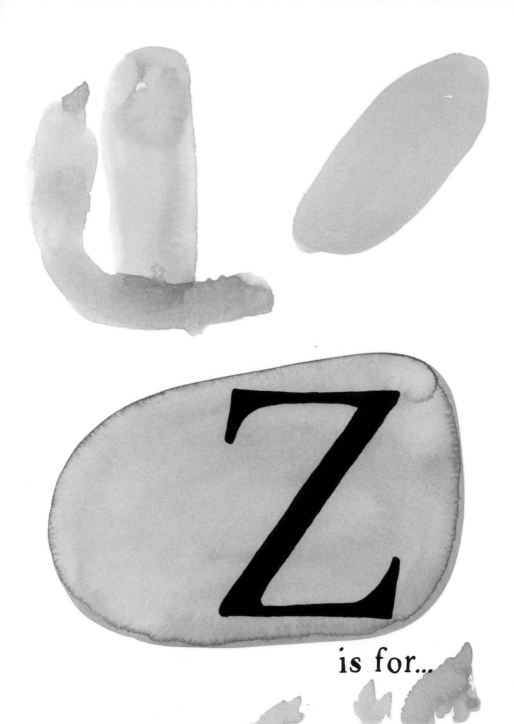

Z

is for...

Zoetic

Zoetic means "of or relating to life." Isn't that what it's all about?

Steinbeck said, "We are no longer perfect, so we can be good." We believe that in letting go of perfection, we can be free.

Being free means free to fuck up. Free to get run down, fall over, and drag yourself up off the floor. It means finding ways to soothe your aching body, to calm your mind, and, for moments at a time, to remember who you are. It means forgiving your mothers, and forgiving yourself. Putting down your addictions because you'd rather stay alive. Choosing every day to love the same person or people, knowing that they, like you, aren't perfect. Knowing that time spent loving someone is more powerful than all the mistakes you make together.

Being free hurts. The medicine is knowing this: You won't ever be able to fix everything that's broken. You can't take all the pain away. What you can do is keep finding ways to become more curious about the pain. Lean into ways to become a little softer, a little more tender, a little more alive, despite the pain. And that's enough.

RESOURCES

For help with substance abuse and recovery

SAMHSA's National Helpline (1-800-662-HELP) is a free, confidential, twenty-four-hour treatment referral and information service. We also recommend checking out Alcoholics Anonymous (www.aa.org) or Narcotics Anonymous (https://www.na.org/).

For help finding cost-effective, local therapy

Visit Open Path Collective (openpathcollective.org).

Traditional Chinese Medicine Resources

We recommend the book *Between Heaven and Earth: A Guide to Chinese Medicine* by Harriet Beinfield, L.Ac., and Efrem Korngold, L.Ac, OMD. Also visit the People's Organization of Community Acupuncture (https://pocacoop.com).

Herbal Resources

The book *Bloom & Thrive: Essential Healing Herbs and Flowers* by Brigit Anna McNeill. For products, try Frontier Natural Products Co-op (Frontiercoop.com, 1-800-669-3275); Healing Spirits Herb Farm (healingspiritsherbfarm.com, 607-566-2701). Also check out Stephanie Portell's Plant Medicine Master List (stephanieportell.com).

Ancestors
Genevieve Slonim
Birth of a Mama
Instagram: @birthofamama

Adaptogens

For further reading, we recommend the book *The First Forty Days* by Heng Ou, a text that focuses on postpartum health and includes recipes to support anyone's well-being or recovery from illness.

Antiracism and Decolonized Healing

These are human beings and works that have transformed our lives, and deepened our ability to love and care for ourselves and our community.

Books

Birthing Justice, edited by Julia Chinyere Oparah and Alicia D. Bonaparte

The Body Is Not an Apology, by Sonya Renee Taylor

Eloquent Rage, by Brittney Cooper

Emergent Strategy, by adrienne maree brown

Questions for Ada, by Ijeoma Umebinyuo

The Radical Doula Guide, by Miriam Zoila Pérez

Radical Reproductive Justice, by Loretta J. Ross, Lynn Roberts, Erika Derkas, Whitney Peoples, and Pamela Bridgewater Toure

So You Want to Talk About Race, by Ijeoma Oluo

When They Call You a Terrorist, by Patrisse Khan-Cullors and Asha Bandele

Films

13th, directed by Ava DuVernay, 2016

Black Art: In the Absence of Light, directed by Sam Pollard, 2021

Healers, Educators, and Organizations

Abide Women's Health Services
www.abidewomen.org
Instagram: @abide_women

Ancient Song Doula Services
www.ancientsongdoulaservices.com
Instagram: @ancientsong

Black Mamas Matter Alliance
blackmamasmatter.org
Instagram: @blackmamasmatter

Black Women's Blueprint
www.blackwomensblueprint.org
Instagram: @blackwomensblueprint

BX Rebirth
https://www.bxrebirth.org/
Instagram: @Bxrebirth

Erika Davis—Whole Body Pregnancy, LLC
www.wholebodypregnancy.com
Instagram: @_wholebodypregnancy_

Flora Pacha—aka the Loba Loca Shares
www.patreon.com/florapacha
Instagram: @flora.pacha

Leesa Renée Hall
leesareneehall.com
Instagram: @leesareneehall

Mayte Noguez—the Womb Doula
www.patreon.com/maytethewombdoula
Instagram: @maytethewombdoula

Montse Olmos
www.patreon.com/Mujer_dela_tierra
Instagram: @mujer_dela_tierra/

The Nap Ministry
thenapministry.wordpress.com
Instagram: @thenapministry

Partera Midwifery
Instagram: @parteramidwifery

Racha Tahani Lawler, CPM, LM
www.crimsonfig.com
Instagram: @crimson_fig

Rachel Cargle
rachelcargle.com
Instagram: @rachel.cargle

Rowen White
sierraseeds.org/rowens-story
Instagram: @rowenwhite

SisterSong—the National Women of Color Reproductive Collective
www.sistersong.net
Instagram: @sistersong_woc

Stephanie Mitchell, DNP, CNM—aka Dr. Midwife
thebirthsanctuary.com
Instagram: @doctor_midwife

Sumi's Touch—aka Sumayyah Franklin
sumistouch.com
Instagram: @sumistouch

Tiny & Brave Holistic Services—aka Barbara Verneus
tinyandbrave.com
Instagram: @tinyandbrave

ACKNOWLEDGMENTS

Our biggest thanks is to Nina Shield and the incredible team at Penguin Random House (especially Hannah Steigmeyer, Jess Morphew, Megan Newman, Laura Corless, and Marian Lizzi) for deftly guiding this book into the world. Thanks also to Paul Lucas at Janklow & Nesbit and Reiko Davis at DeFiore and Company.

ERIN:
Kate, you are a force of nature and one of my biggest inspirations, always. Thank you for trusting, honoring, and nurturing me. Thank you for loving me before I learned to love myself.

Mary Karr: Thank you for teaching me what I know about generosity, compassion, humility, and service. Thanks for always answering the phone, particularly all the times I was scream-crying from a back corner of Duane Reade about how impossible it is to be a mom. You're one of the greatest moms of my life.

Thanks to the ragtag crew of geniuses without whom I couldn't have survived the last few years: Leslie, Cait, Melissa, Jana, Afaa, Benjamin, Betsy, Bernardo, Chase, Chris, Kurt, Jamie, Joy, Kaveh, Krissy, Zach, Scotty, Dev, and Phil. Thanks to all my beautiful, life-affirming friends: Adriana Pentz, Shannon Frank, Jenny Edelstein, Blythe Adamson, Cennet Braun, Sarah Paule, and Indira Ranganathan. Thank you Rain, Dee, and Alex for opening your lives to me.

Thanks to Mariah Adcox, Caleigh Farragher, and Forsyth Harmon, who've taught me so much about what it means to care for others. I love you big big.

Thanks to my parents and grandparents, Florence Acker Williams in particular, my blueprint for Susan.

Kyle: Thank you for loving me despite and through the weird and inconvenient manifestations of my PTSD. Thank you for being an incredible dad to our Lu.

Lucy, Lucy, Lucy: You've challenged me in ways I didn't think I'd survive. You scooped out my insides and filled them up with what's spilled out on these pages.

Thank you for teaching me how to take care. Thank you for being the crystal queen of my heart.

KATE:

Thank you to Erin, for being one of my favorite living artists. Your art creates worlds: For me, it created a world where this book could exist. Thank you for being my book doula and always, for being my mom.

Thank you to the ones I love that helped me envision what this book was for:

To Lisa and Jackson. To Whitney and Barrett and Baby Girl. To Jessica and Jamie. To Jeanie and Jonah, Gavin and Oliver. To Barbara and Glorious-Zoelle. To Karen and Ty. To Mayte and Xhavier, Evan, Violeta and Butti. To Grammy and Kelli and Lacey, Lesli, Leah, Lane and Luke. To JenJo and Kaleb, Hannah, and Ezrah. To Katie and Joshua, Caleb, and Jesse. To Sam and Charlie and Aubree. To Kelli and Maggie. To Loba and Scrimpy. To Melissa and Mckayla, Mason, Olivia, Victoria and Gabriel. To Samantha and Pascale and Sebastien. To Christina and Adeline and Henry. To Stephanie and Elijah, Wendy, and Brigid. To Amanda and Rocco Boone and Arlo Graham. To my sister, Alice, for reminding me to love my inner child. To Sarah, for attending all my poetry slams. A Odilia Raxjal, *por todo lo que eres*. To Dad and Irene, for helping me follow the string back. To Don and Janiece, thank you for loving me. To Erin and Lucy. To all of my mothers, including my first one. Thanks for making me laugh, Mom, and teaching me to fight.

Thank you to Tusca, who taught me how to care for myself so that I could be the mama you deserve. Thank you to Mike—for loving me beyond my wildest dreams, and for giving me a future I can hope for. I love you.

NOTES

ix In *The Body Keeps the Score*: Bessel van der Kolk, *The Body Keeps the Score: Brain, Mind, and Body in the Healing of Trauma* (New York: Penguin Books, 2015), 30.

2 "Most of us think of trauma": Resmaa Menakem, *My Grandmother's Hands: Racialized Trauma and the Pathway to Mending Our Hearts and Bodies* (Las Vegas: Central Recovery Press, 2017), 37.

9 Anger can be medicine: Brittney Cooper, *Eloquent Rage: A Black Feminist Discovers Her Superpower* (New York: Picador, 2019).

11 systemic racism wreaks havoc: Resmaa Menakem, *My Grandmother's Hands: Racialized Trauma and the Pathway to Mending Our Hearts and Bodies* (Las Vegas: Central Recovery Press, 2017), 37.

12 "Healing trauma involves": Resmaa Menakem, *My Grandmother's Hands: Racialized Trauma and the Pathway to Mending Our Hearts and Bodies* (Las Vegas: Central Recovery Press, 2017), 165.

39 Suffering is a door: See the poem by Louise Glück in *The Wild Iris* (New York: Harper-Collins, 2014). See also "Surrender" (page 133).

92 from Allen Ginsberg to: Dana Ward, "A Kentucky of Mothers." *Pen America*, 2014. pen .org/a-kentucky-of-mothers.

93 In *Women Who Run with the Wolves*: Clarissa Pinkola Estés: *Women Who Run with the Wolves* (New York: Ballantine Books, 1992), 47–48.

95 Yoga in particular: Autumn M. Gallegos, Hugh F. Crean, Wilfred R. Pigeon, and Kathi L. Heffner, "Meditation and Yoga for Posttraumatic Stress Disorder: A Meta-Analytic Review of Randomized Controlled Trials." *Clinical Psychology Review* 58 (2017): 115–24. doi.10.1016/j.cpr.2017.10.004.

95 Running and other vigorous exercise: Nicole J. Hegberg, Jasmeet P. Hayes, and Scott M. Hayes. "Exercise Intervention in PTSD: A Narrative Review and Rationale for Implementation." *Frontiers in Psychiatry* 10 (2019). doi.10.3389/fpsyt.2019.00133.

111 "Rather than indulge or reject": Pema Chödrön, *When Things Fall Apart* (Boulder, CO: Shambhala, 2016), 16.

111 "lean in when we feel": Ibid., 13.

112 "The Voice of God": Mary Karr, *Tropic of Squalor: Poems* (New York: HarperCollins, 2020), 47.

118 "After all, if Black women": Keeanga-Yamahtta Taylor, *How We Get Free: Black Feminism and the Combahee River Collective* (Chicago: Haymarket Books, 2012), 22–23.

118 "Caring for myself is not": Audre Lorde, *A Burst of Light and Other Essays* (New York: Ixia Press, 2017), 140.

127 Volunteering can decrease: Jill Suttie, "Staying Sober through Service," *Greater Good Magazine.* The Greater Good Science Center at the University of California, Berkeley, March 13, 2012. greatergood.berkeley.edu/article/item/staying_sober_through_service.

134 "At the end of my suffering": Louise Glück, *The Wild Iris* (New York: HarperCollins, 2014).

150 Vicarious trauma is defined: Mehlmann-Wicks, Jackie. "Vicarious Trauma: Signs and Strategies for Coping." British Medical Association, September 7, 2020. www.bma.org.uk /advice-and-support/your-wellbeing/vicarious-trauma/vicarious-trauma-signs-and-strategies -for-coping.

150 People who regularly empathize: Graham James, "Identify Stress and Vicarious, Secondary, Indirect Trauma in Nurses." *Ausmed*, April 18, 2020. www.ausmed.com/cpd/articles /stress-trauma-nurses&sa=D&source=docs&ust=1635913688248000&usg=AOvVaw3ut5SCO9 buFiHgkGlQgATZ.

152 Brené Brown defines: Brené Brown, *Dare to Lead* (New York: Random House, 2018), 20.